Don't Be . . . Taken Hostage!

DON'T BE . . .
TAKEN HOSTAGE

A Workbook to Help You Survive Your Adolescent

John Jensen, M.Ed., L.A.C.

Professional Resource
Network Publishing

Edited by:
Carol Kapaun Ratchenski

Cover Design:
Robert Washnieski

Typeset and Layout:
Mary Hapala

Illustrations:
Michael Joachim

Published by:
Professional Resource Network
Fargo, North Dakota 58106

ISBN 0-9628996-0-7

Dedicated To:

My wife Lori, for without her love and support this project would not be a reality.

To my children, Phillip, Jessica, and Joseph, who have taught me how to be a parent.

To Mary Lou, who through her wisdom and friendship, has taught me how to be a family therapist.

To Julie and Melody, two tough and talented counselors who taught me how to be a supervisor.

And to Jackie, who taught me what it really means to be a counselor.

With Love and Gratitude
To Each of You!

The objective of this workbook is to introduce you to some basic concepts relating to adolescent behavior and drug abuse. While intended to cover drugs abused by adolescents, it does not contain a complete listing of all potentially abused drugs. Along with the drugs of abuse are descriptions of adolescent drug affected behavior and warning signs that an adolescent may be harmfully involved with alcohol/drugs. The workbook also covers what to do if you suspect alcohol/drug use and strategies parents and professionals can use to avoid being taken hostage by an adolescent's behavior or alcohol/drug use.

Dear Reader,

This workbook developed out of my work with parents and adolescents involved in inpatient and outpatient drug abuse programs. I have found that many parents have little understanding of the adolescent drug scene, and even less understanding of drugs. Often, parents can clearly describe behaviors that are causing concern, but cannot describe their adolescent's chemical useage.

The workbook is based on my working experience with families and their drug abusing adolescents. It is also based on questions that I posed to kids and what they told me about their drug use, as well as from a review of the current literature concerning drugs of abuse and specifically adolescent drug use.

Information is a powerful tool in the fight against adolescent drug abuse and adolescent acting out behavior. The workbook is intended to be a source of information for parents. As parents, the better informed we are the more parenting alternatives we have.

The workbook is designed to give the reader a basic understanding of adolescent chemical use and the drugs often found on the street. It is not intended to make the reader an expert. The workbook is designed in sections to make reading easier. Each chapter challenges you to complete a series of activities designed to help you understand and respond to adolescent alcohol/drug abuse and behavior problems.

My hope is that you find this workbook informative, as well as challenging. My intent is not only to educate, but also to open up new avenues of thought.

TABLE OF CONTENTS

Bill of Rights for Parents

AS A PARENT, I HAVE . . .

- The right to have my needs be as important as the needs of my adolescent
- The right to makes mistakes
- The right to refuse the requests of my adolescent without feeling guilty or selfish
- The right to say no and not have to defend my decisions to my adolescent
- The right to express my opinion
- The right to ask questions and seek information about my adolescent
- The right to change my mind
- The right to feel and express feelings, including anger as long as I don't violate the rights of others
- The right to be treated as a capable parent and to be taken seriously
- The right to be treated with respect by my adolescent
- The right to have my property and possessions left alone
- The right to expect my adolescent to take responsibility for his/her behavior
- The right to refuse to let my adolescent swear at me or verbally or physically abuse me
- The right to ask for help from others if I feel threatened
- The right to be safe in my own home

Where Do You Stand On The Issue?

We learn to be parents from our own parents. In turn, we teach our children how to parent. Family attitudes and values are passed on from one generation to another. Before moving on, take time to examine your own family attitudes. Respond to the following questions as thoroughly as you can. Ask family members what their attitudes are.

✍ What is/was your parents' attitude toward recreational alcohol/drug use?

____

____

____

____

____

____

✍ What is your attitude toward recreational alcohol/drug use?

____

____

____

____

____

____

✍ What is your children's attitude toward recreational alcohol/drug use?

____

____

____

____

____

✎ Place an ✗ in the position on each scale that most closely matches your opinion.

➡ A. Chemical dependency is a disease.

1	2	3	4	5
strongly agree				*strongly disagree*

➡ B. Parents can teach their children to drink responsibly.

1	2	3	4	5
strongly agree				*strongly disagree*

➡ C. It's OK for an adolescent to experiment with alcohol.

1	2	3	4	5
strongly agree				*strongly* disagree

➡ D. Drinking is a normal part of life.

1	2	3	4	5
strongly agree				*strongly disagree*

➡ E. Alcohol is not as bad as drugs.

1	2	3	4	5
strongly agree				*strongly disagree*

➡ F. Stopping chemical abuse is the responsibility of government.

1	2	3	4	5
strongly agree				*strongly* disagree

Suggested Responses

Sample Question: Chemical dependency is a disease.

Suggested Answer: Strongly agree

The World Health Organization and the American Medical Association have recognized chemical dependency as a disease. Chemical dependency is a progressive, chronic and fatal disease that has a set of observable and predictable symptoms. The prescription for arresting the disease is abstinence from alcohol/drug use. The person experiencing the disease is never cured.

Sample Question: Parents can teach their children to drink responsibly.

Suggested Answer: Strongly disagree

Parents can teach their children to drink. Parents cannot teach their children to drink responsibly. Because alcohol clouds judgment, once an adolescent begins to drink, they lose the ability to make responsible decisions. Research shows that the younger the adolescent when they begin using chemicals, the higher at risk they are for chemical dependency.

Sample Question: It's OK for an adolescent to experiment with alcohol.

Suggested Answer: Strongly disagree

Alcohol use has a dramatic and profound impact on the physical, emotional, psychological, and spiritual growth of an adolescent. For that reason, it is unacceptable for adults to sanction alcohol/drug use by adolescents. Research shows that the younger you are when you begin alcohol/drug use, the higher at risk you are for becoming chemically dependent.

Sample Question: Drinking is a normal part of life.

Suggested Answer: Strongly disagree

Advertising and media portray drinking as normal, even important part of life. Yet more and more groups are showing us that life without alcohol can be fun and fulfilling. We need to look at the messages we give young people about the role of alcohol in our lives. They learn from us through imitation and role modeling.

Sample Question: Alcohol is not as bad as drugs.

Suggested Answer: Strongly disagree

Alcohol is a drug. The damage that alcohol abuse creates has been downplayed largely in part because it is a legal substance that has been with us for centuries. When comparing drugs, a number of factors must be taken into consideration, such as dose, length of use, concentration, social risks, and the individual's psychological, emotional and physical risk factors.

Sample Question: Stopping chemical abuse is the responsibility of government.

Suggested Answer: Strongly disagree

Government alone does not have the resources to combat this problem. It takes the effort of each individual to address this issue. We need to examine our attitudes and what we teach our children. We need to look at how we cope with stress as well as how we use our leisure time. Attitudes need to change. It is time to stop laughing at the drunk at the party and start reaching out to help fight a serious and tragic disease.

The Enemy

Drugs of Abuse

The purpose of this section is to help you understand specific drugs which are being abused by an increasing number of adolescents in our society. Before we take an indepth look at the specific drugs of abuse and the chemical families that they come from, we will define some important concepts that you need to be acquainted with.

What is a drug?

A drug is any chemical substance that when introduced into the body alters the way the body functions. This is a very broad definition that can even include food substances. Our bodies are like magnificient chemistry sets. We add chemicals to our bodies on a regular basis and the body eliminates chemicals on a regular basis. The body has a natural ability to monitor and regulate itself chemically.

By ingesting certain chemical substances, we can alter the balance and change the body's ability to regulate itself. By changing the chemical balance within the brain, we can produce different effects and emotions. Some of these changes can be pleasant and rewarding. Others can be emotionally painful and frightening.

For the purpose of this discussion, the focus will be on drugs that fit into the category of mood altering substances. These chemical substances affect the central nervous system in some manner and thus change the way we feel. For some individuals, this change of mood is desireable. This leads to a pattern of abuse which can become psychological and physical dependence.

Dependence falls in two categories, physical and psychological. Adolescents often fall into the category of psychological dependence, rather than that of physical dependence (although it is not uncommon in a treatment center to see 17 or 18-year-old addicts that have progressed to the point where they are experiencing serious physical withdrawal symptomology).

Psychological Dependence

Psychological drug dependence is the most difficult to deal with, because it affects the emotional and intellectual processes. The drug becomes a coping mechanism. Adolescents depend on the drug to help them deal with problems and emotional pain. The emotional experiences of the psychologically dependent adolescent become quite narrow. Later as their emotional growth is stunted and chemical use persists, psychological dependence grows, mood swings and fluctuations in attitude become pronounced. Parents begin to see adolescents as irritable and moody and do not understand the source of these emotional changes. For the adolescent, increased stress brings on increased usage.

Physical Dependence

Physical dependence is defined as the body's growing dependence on the presence of a drug to maintain a specific level of physical functioning. When denied the drug, the body goes through a period of re-adjustment as it attempts to compensate for the loss of the drug. Physical dependence can be identified through two characteristics which produce a set of predictable symptoms: tolerance increase and withdrawal symptomology.

Tolerance is a process where it takes an increased amount of a chemical substance to achieve a particular point of intoxication. The body's ability to tolerate certain chemical substances changes as over a period of time the body's response to the drug gradually decreases. Therefore, it takes more of a chemical substance to reach the same point of intoxication.

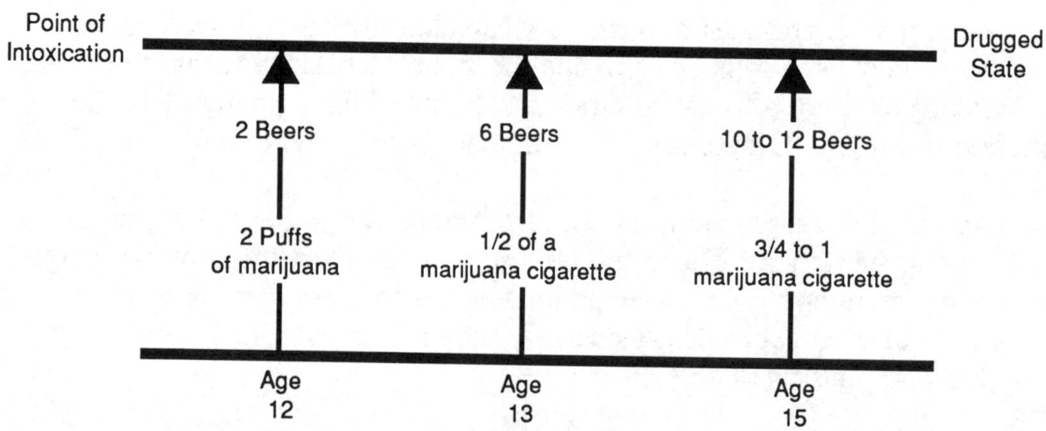

This graph illustrates the concept of tolerance. The numbers used to represent age and amount of drug used are arbitrary and will vary from person to person. With adolescents, rate of growth, body size, and body weight will influence tolerance change. An adolescent who grows six inches and gains forty pounds will obviously be able to drink more without experiencing a significant change in the effects they feel.

This is an important concept because while most adolescents drink more or use more of a chemical substance to achieve a greater state of intoxication, they do not experience an actual tolerance increase. When working with adolescents, it is important to be careful to differentiate between levels of intoxication and tolerance increase.

Point of intoxication is defined as the point where a person begins to experience the effects of a mood altering chemical substance. This is the point at which we can detect that there is a physical impact of the chemical on the body. In working with adolescents, point of intoxication (or as the kids like to refer to it, a buzz) is defined as that point at which you may begin to feel light headed, slur your speech, feel thick tongued, or wobble when you get up and walk.

Physical withdrawal occurs when the body has adapted to the chemical substance being present on a regular basis and upon cessation of chemical useage, has to re-adapt itself to a non-drug state. This readjustment produces a physically uncomfortable set of symptoms which can include shakes, tremors, delirium tremors, hallucinations, convulsions, and, with some chemicals, death.

Origins of Drugs

When we look at the origins of drugs, we find that there are three basic origins: natural, semi-synthetic and synthetic.

Natural drugs are those found in nature and do not require any changes before they can be used.

Semi-synthetic drugs are those drugs which are manufactured in the laboratory from natural substances.

Synthetic drugs are those which are manufactured in the laboratory from man-made chemical compounds.

Unit Review - I.

Circle the correct answer . . .

1 Mood altering chemical substances affect:

A. The spinal cord
B. The central nervous system
C. The kidneys
D. The spleen

2 Dependence falls into two categories: physical and psychological.

A. True
B. False

3 Physical dependence can be identified by two characteristics. They are:

A. Tolerance and frequency
B. Frequency and abstinence
C. Withdrawal and abstinence
D. Tolerance and withdrawal

4 Tolerance is the nervous system's ability to:

A. Handle more alcohol/drugs
B. Function without alcohol/drugs
C. Handle less alcohol/drugs
D. Withdraw from alcohol/drugs

5 Withdrawal is the nervous system's response to the presence of a drug after physical dependence has occurred.

A. True
B. False

6 Natural drugs are those drugs which:

A. Have no preservatives
B. Are found in nature
C. Are made in the lab
D. Are found in a health food store

7 Synthetic drugs are those drugs which:

A. Have preservatives
B. Are found in nature
C. Are made in the lab
D. Are found in a health food store

8 Semi-synthetic drugs are those drugs which:

A. Have preservatives
B. Are found in nature and then processed in the lab
C. Are made in the lab
D. Are found in a health food store

Answers found on Page 203

Depressants

Depressants are a class of drugs capable of depressing the central nervous system. They can produce decreased inhibitions, a sense of euphoria and well being, as well as a slowed heart rate, and decreased blood pressure. In large doses, depressants are capable of producing coma and death.

Depressants

Drug Name	Street Name	What Does It Look Like?	Method of Use	What To Look For	Dangers and Harmful Effects
Alcohol: Beer Wine Liquor	Booze, Suds, Liquor, Spirits, Barley Pop, Brew, Liquid Courage, Juice, Hooch, Sauce	Clear or colored liquid	Swallowed in liquid form	Intoxicated behavior, slurred speech, impaired judgment, impaired coordination, nausea, vomiting	Physical and psychological dependence Ulcers of throat and stomach Damage to the heart and liver Death from accidents Death from overdose
Barbiturates: Pentobarbital Secobarbital Amobarbital Tuinal Amytal Phenobarbital	Downers, Blues, Yellows, Yellow Jackets, Purple Hearts, Red, Barbs, Rainbows, Nebbies, Green Dragons, Red Devils	Red, red and blue, blue, yellow capsules, white tablets, or clear liquid for injection	Taken orally or injected	Intoxicated behavior Constricted pupils Slurred speech Impaired judgment Impaired coordination Needle marks	Physical and psychological dependence Infection from needle use Severe withdrawal symtoms Death from accidents Coma or death from overdose
Methaqualone	Quaaludes, Ludes, Sopors	Tablets	Taken orally or crushed and inhaled nasally	Behavior that resembles alcohol intoxication	Physical and psychological dependence Severe withdrawal Coma or death from overdose
Minor Tranquilizers: Valium Librium Dalmane Chloral Hydrate Serax Equanil/Miltown	Tranks, Downs, Sleeping Pills, Sleepers	Tablet, Capsule, or Liquid form for injection	Taken orally, injected, or crushed and inhaled nasally	Similar to Barbiturates except less intense Impaired coordination	Physical and psychological dependence Infection from needle use Withdrawal symptoms similar to barbiturates Death from accidents

BEER
BEER
Q

Alcohol

Historical Perspective **–** Considered the oldest drug, alcohol is also the most widely used drug. Its use in ancient rituals, which marked important events in life, is well documented. Ancient societies worshipped various gods of wine that resided over events such as war, birth and death. The use of alcohol eventually found its way into everyday religious practices. The bible documents rituals of sacrifice that included wine. In the tenth century, an arabic physician discovered the process of distilling alcohol, thus increasing the percentage of alcohol contained in beverages. In the early years of distillation, alcohol was used primarily as a medicine and cure for various ailments.

In the sixteenth century, alcohol gained in popularity as a drink. Alcohol came to the United States with the colonists and its use was unrestricted until the prohibition years of the 1920's. During this time, the manufacture, possession, and sale of alcohol was prohibited. After the depression years of the 1920's and 1930's, alcohol was legalized and regulated by the United States government. Now a major source of tax revenue for the Federal government, alcohol is the most widely accepted form of recreation in this country. Unfortunately, it is also the most destructive form of recreation we know.

Origin **–** Ethyl alcohol is produced when any mixture of watery fruits and vegetable juices are allowed to stand in warm temperatures for a period of time. The sugar and starches in the fruits and vegetables are exposed to yeast spores which reside naturally in the air. The yeast spores produce an enzyme causing the mixture to ferment, converting the sugar to alcohol. This process can be duplicated in a controlled environment, and the alcohol content in the mixtures can be increased through a distillation process.

Street Names **–** Booze, Suds, Liquor, Spirits, Barley Pop, Brew, Liquid Courage, Juice, Hooch, Sauce

Route of Administration **–** Alcohol is ingested orally in a liquid form called beer, wine, or hard liquor. As the user is ingesting alcohol, it is quickly absorbed into the blood stream through the lining of the mouth, throat and stomach. Alcohol is easily absorbed into the tissues of the body and as it moves through the blood stream crosses the blood brain barrier affecting brain function.

Effects **–** Alcohol is a depressant drug. At low doses, alcohol has the ability to depress the inhibitory nerve center of the brain. As the inhibitory nerve center is depressed, the alcohol user feels a release of excitement and stimulation. This experience is short lived as the concentration of alcohol in the brain increases and the body systems of the user are depressed.

The effect of alcohol on the user varies with the amount of alcohol consumed, the concentration of alcohol consumed, and the amount of time within which the alcohol is consumed. It is important to know that 1/2 oz. of "hard" liquor (86 proof) is equal to 6 oz. of wine, or 12 oz. of beer. The liver is able to remove alcohol from the body at a rate of 1/2 oz. of pure alcohol every hour. Any amount of alcohol consumed above this amount remains in the blood stream providing a continuous effect on the user.

What To Look For **–** The user will have a distinct odor of alcohol on their breath and clothes. Alcohol produces nausea, vomiting, double vision, staggering or unsteady gait, emotional changes, loss of motor coordination, delayed reaction time to external stimulus, and unconsciousness.

Long Term Effects **–** The long term use of alcohol can lead to a number of serious harmful physical effects on the user. Among these are liver disease, heart disease resulting from damage of the heart muscle, ulcers of the throat and stomach, loss of weight, anemia and a decreased immunity to infection and disease, hepatitis, and pancreatitis. There is no system of the body that escapes the destructive forces of alcohol.

One effect associated with heavy or continuous drinking is the "blackout". A blackout is a period of amnesia where the alcohol user cannot remember events that occur while they are under the influence of the drug. The person who experiences a blackout will not remember part or all of an event because memory storage in the brain is interrupted. The blank space in the memory may be partial or total.

Effects of Overdose **–** Alcohol is an irritant and in large quantities can produce nausea and vomiting. Alcohol is also an anesthetic drug that is capable of producing a state of unconsciousness. It is not used as an anesthetic drug because it is unpredictable and the amount of alcohol needed to produce the anesthetic effect is dangerously close to the amount needed to produce coma and death. Alcohol has the ability to depress the vital center of the brain which controls critical body functions such as heart rate, breathing and blood pressure. If the brain and body systems are depressed enough, the user may experience coma or death.

Withdrawal Symptoms **–** It is clearly documented that alcohol produces both physical and psychological dependence. Tolerance can occur with long term use of low doses of alcohol, or with short term use of high doses of alcohol. Physical withdrawal symptoms include: anxiety, insomnia, irritability, sweats, nightmares, shakes and tremors, confusion, delirium, headaches, hallucinations, and seizures. In some cases, withdrawal from alcohol can lead to death.

Special Concerns **–** When alcohol is combined with other depressant drugs (such as members of the barbiturate family), the effects can be fatal. The two drugs multiply against each other and depress the brain systems in an unpredictable fashion. Research shows that most hospital emergency room visits that involve alcohol, involve alcohol in combination with other drugs.

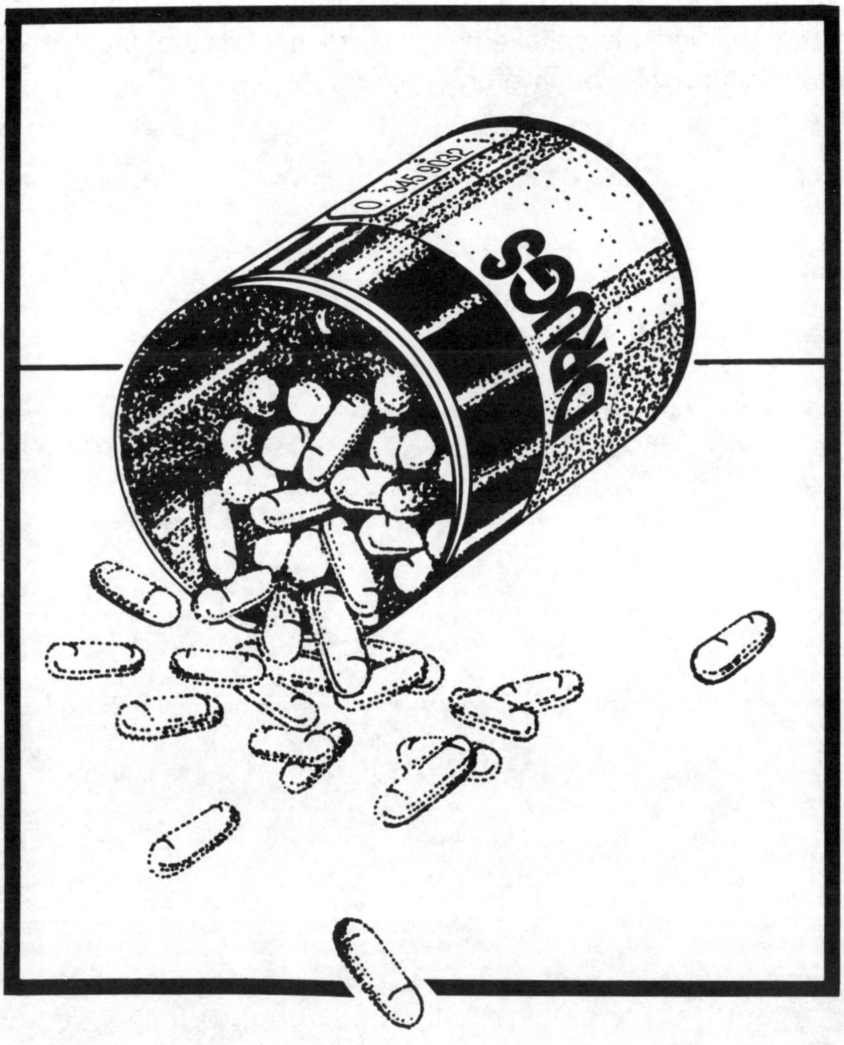
DRUGS
0 345 9032

Barbiturates and Minor Tranquilizers

Historical Perspective **–** The oldest of the synthetic depressants appeared in 1862 with the synthesis of Chloral Hydrate. It was first used for sedation and inducing sleep. In the early 1900's, barbital was introduced giving physicians a drug that could achieve the full range of depressant effects in patients. The addictive qualities of barbiturates were quickly identified and science continued its search for safe non-habit forming depressant drugs. With the progression of Psychiatric medicine in the 1950's, came the advent of minor tranquilizers which were soon hailed as the depressant of the new age.

Minor tranquilizers such as benzodiazepines (i.e. Valium) were widely prescribed in the late 1950's and 1960's before the addictive qualities of these drugs were fully known. Then, Valium was the most widely prescribed drug in the United States. These drugs are still widely prescribed although the Federal government is closely monitoring their manufacture and distribution. Methaqualone (Quaalude), the most popular barbiturate drug of abuse, was first introduced into the United States in 1965. It quickly gained a reputation for producing a quality high, as well as severe addiction, and was widely copied on the black market. Though the manufacturer withdrew the drug from the market in 1983, even today copies of methaqualone are seized by law enforcement personnel in drug raids.

Origins **–** Barbiturates are synthetic drugs that depress the central nervous system, thus reducing anxiety and tension. Minor tranquilizers are other synthetic depressant drugs used to calm, relax and decrease anxiety. Barbiturates are far more potent than minor tranquilizers. Yet, both have a number of medical uses. They are used to treat anxiety disorders, reduce tension and blood pressure, treat ulcers, and epilepsy.

Street Names **–** Downers, Tranks, Reds, Blues, Yellows, Yellow Jackets, Rainbows, Ludes, Barbs, Sleepers, Sleeping Pills, Bluebirds, Christmas trees, Nebbies, Green Dragons, Red Devils

***Route of Administration* –** Barbiturates and minor tranquilizers are found in tablet, capsule, powder and liquid form. The most common route of administration is oral ingestion; but they may also be snorted (inhaled nasally) in a powder form produced by crushing the tablet form of the drug. These drugs may also be injected directly into the vein (mainlining). Effects of barbiturates last anywhere from 1 to 16 hours depending on the type, amount, and potency. Effects of minor tranquilizers may last anywhere from 4 to 8 hours depending on the type, amount, and potency.

***Effects* –** Barbiturates and minor tranquilizers produce effects similar to that of alcohol, varying from person to person and from time to time in the same individual. In small doses, barbiturates and minor tranquilizers produce a feeling of well being and decreased anxiety. In large doses, barbiturates and minor tranquilizers produce a euphoric state of intoxication marked by impaired motor coordination, judgment, cognition, disorientated behavior, and slurred speech.

***What To Look For* –** Intoxicated behavior resembling that of alcohol intoxication without the odor of alcohol is an indicator of barbiturate or minor tranquilizer use. Look for uncoordinated behavior with slurred speech and disorientated or confused thinking. Barbiturate and minor tranquilizer users will also demonstrate poor hygiene and nutritional habits. They are apathetic, unmotivated and will not participate in the normal social activities of someone their age.

***Long Term Effects* –** Barbiturates and minor tranquilizers when used over an extended period of time produce apathy and lethargy. Users begin to neglect their personal appearance and nutritional needs, generally suffer from vitamin deficiencies and problems related to liver dysfunction. Barbiturate users who choose to inject the drug are subject to collapsed veins, skin abscesses, lesions and a host of infections, especially if the needle is shared with another addict. Shared needles are also responsible for the spread of disease such as hepatitis and AIDS.

***Effects of Overdose* –** Barbiturates and minor tranquilizers act in a similar manner to alcohol in high doses. Symptoms of barbiturates and minor tranquilizer overdose include dilated pupils, cold clammy skin, shallow respiration accompanied by rapid and weak pulse. An overdose of barbiturates or minor tranquilizers is a life threatening medical emergency. In large doses, barbiturates and minor tranquilizers may lead to a collapse of the functioning of the vital center of the brain causing coma or death.

***Withdrawal Symptoms* –** Barbiturates produce both a strong psychological and physical dependence. Minor tranquilizers are also capable of producing physical and psychological dependence but at a slower rate than barbiturates. Withdrawal from barbiturates and minor tranquilizers is a dangerous process and should be done under the supervision of a physician. Withdrawal symptoms include anxiety and irritability, a disruption of sleep patterns, tremors and shakes, confusion or delirium, and convulsions. Withdrawal from barbiturates can also include muscle twitching, headaches, nausea, weakness, a sudden drop in blood pressure, and in some cases, death. Withdrawal symptoms usually reach climax within 2 to 3 days after the cessation of drug use. Though with some of the short acting barbiturates, withdrawal symptoms may not reach their peak for 7 to 10 days after cessation.

***Special Concerns* –** When depressant drugs (such as members of the barbiturate family) are combined with alcohol, the effects can be fatal. The two drugs multiply against each other and depress the brain systems in an unpredictable fashion.

Opiates

Opiates are a class of drugs capable of depressing the central nervous system producing a sense of euphoria and well being, relieving pain and inducing sleep. In large doses, opiates are capable of depressing the vital functions of the body and producing coma or death.

Opiates

Drug Name	Street Name	What Does It Look Like?	Method of Use	What To Look For	Dangers and Harmful Effects
Opium	O, Big O, Oppie	Dark brown chunks Powder	Smoked or eaten	With narcotic use, the drug will leave the individual appearing drunk or intoxicated. Will appear lethargic and drowsy and includes: Confusion Impaired coordination Impaired judgment Look for needle marks, needles, or candle, spoon and cotton used to heat drug to liquefy. In high doses, will have cold clammy skin and shallow breathing.	Severe physical and psychological addiction with severe withdrawal symptoms. Loss of appetite Malnutrition, Anemia Coma or death from overdose Needle users risk infections such as hepatitis and AIDS. Needle use can also lead to skin abscesses, lesions, and collapsed veins.
Heroin	Junk, Smack, Horse, H., Big H, Brown Sugar, Mud, Black Tar	White to dark powder Tar like subtance	Smoked, injected, snorted (inhaled through nasal passages)		
Morphine	Dreamer, Junk, Cube, Morf, Mud	White crystals Injectable solution Hypodermic tablets	Smoked Injected Taken orally		
Methadone	Meth, dope	Injectable solution Tablets, Capsules	Injected Taken orally		
Codeine	School Boy, T's	Dark liquid Tablets, Capsules	Injected Taken orally		
Other Narcotics	Percodan, Talwin Darvon, Percocet Fentanyl, Lomotil Tussionex, Demerol	Tablets, Capsules, Liquid, White Powder	Injected Taken orally Snorted (inhaled through nasal passages)		

The poppy Papaver somniferum is the main source of nonsynthetic narcotics. It is grown in countries around the world including: China, Burma, Mexico, Hungary, Turkey, and Yugoslavia.

The ripe seedpod is incised allowing the milky fluid of the pod to ooze out. The fluid is left to air dry and is then scraped from the seedpod by hand, producing Opium gum. Morphine is the principal constituent of Opium and is one of the most effective drugs known for the relief of pain.

Opiates

Historical Perspective – Opium is another drug that has been around for centuries. It was first used as a remedy for diarrhea and later as a sleep aid. The alkaloids of opium were first isolated from the opium poppy in Europe during the early years of the nineteenth century. Opium use spread in Europe during the eighteenth century before its addictive properties were known. Use of the drug in medicine, as a pain killer, accelerated with the advent of the hypodermic syringe. Addiction to morphine spread across Europe as the result of its use as a pain killer for soldiers wounded in war. This held true in the late 1960's as soldiers who were wounded in Vietnam brought their addiction back to the United States to share it with their family and friends. In the early 1970's, heroin use was considered at crisis proportions as heroin addiction spread in the inner cities of the United States. Since the late 1970's, cocaine (especially crack cocaine) has replaced heroin as the scourge of the country and has become the focus of America's drug war.

Origin – Opiates (narcotic substances) are known for their ability to relieve acute pain and induce sleep. Opium and morphine are derived from the opium poppy grown in the far east. Heroin is produced by chemically treating Morphine. Heroin in a pure form is anywhere from two to six times stronger than Morphine. Synthetic narcotics mimic action of natural opiate substances and are manufactured for medical use under strict Federal control. Methadone, an example of a synthetic narcotic, was originally developed to combat heroin dependence. Methadone does not produce the "high" that heroin produces, but prevents the addict from experiencing uncomfortable withdrawal symptoms. Unfortunately, methadone users develop physical and psychological dependence on the drug.

Street Names –

HEROIN Smack, Horse, Big H, H, Heroina, Junk, Thing, Crap, Shit, Brown, Brown Sugar, Chiva, Mexican Mud, Scag

MORPHINE Cube, Goma, Morf, Morpho, Mud, Dollies, Downtown, Demies, School Boy

Route of Administration – Opiates are found in tablet, capsule, powder and liquid form. The most common route of administration for these drugs is by hypodermic injection. The drug may be placed under the skin with a needle (skin popping) or may be injected directly into the vein (mainlining). The drug may be taken orally in pill form or snorted (inhaled nasally) in a powder form. The drug may also be smoked in a pipe or by spraying it on another smokeable substance (such as marijuana).

Effects – The effects of the drug will depend on the type and the amount taken. Opiate drugs that are illegally manufactured and distributed on the black market vary in strength and purity. These drugs are diluted with fillers to increase the amount available for sale and to increase profits.

Narcotics depress areas of the brain that control anxiety, tension, hunger, thirst, sex drive, and ultimately the vital center of the brain. Narcotic drugs produce a euphoric state that is described by users as a state of tranquility and well being accompanied by a feeling of warmth and a tingling sensation in the abdomen. The drug lasts for several hours and is marked by the users inability to concentrate, impaired coordination, and lethargy described as a dream-like state.

What To Look For – Because the main route of administration is through injection, the user needs to have a syringe and a means to constrict their limbs (tourniquet) to increase the size of blood vein sites on the arms and legs. They may also have a candle, spoon, and cotton for heating and liquefying the drug. The narcotic user may have needle marks or scars on their arms and legs. The user is lethargic and has constricted pupils accompanied by drunken behavior.

Long Term Effects – Long term narcotic users experience malnutrition and anemia. The narcotic drug user does not experience long term negative effects from the drug itself but from the way the drug is used. Needle users are subject to a host of infections, especially if the needle is shared with another addict. Shared needles are also responsible for the spread of disease such as hepatitis and AIDS and needle use can lead to collapsed veins and skin abscesses and lesions.

Effects of Overdose – Narcotic users experience overdose if the drug is stronger than they are accustomed to. An overdose is a serious medical emergency. The drug depresses the vital center of the brain, the respiratory center of the brain and in large enough doses can cause respiratory failure. Symptoms of a narcotic overdose include slow shallow labored breathing, cold clammy skin, constricted pupils, convulsions, and left untreated may lead to coma and death.

Withdrawal Symptoms – Opiates (narcotics) are highly addictive both physically and psychologically. Opiates in some cases produce physical addiction before psychological dependence. The body quickly adapts to the presence of the chemical and begins to to develop tolerance. The chronic opiate user who ceases to use experiences a significant withdrawal process. Withdrawal is categorized by watery eyes, yawning, a runny nose, loss of appetite, irritability, panic, tremors, chills, muscle cramps, sweats, nausea and vomiting.

The withdrawal process begins a few hours after the last dose and will reach its peak somewhere between 24 to 48 hours later. The more serious or uncomfortable symptoms will last up to 10 days. After withdrawal occurs, tolerance to the drug is lost. A dose of the same strength and amount used previous to withdrawal, will produce an overdose.

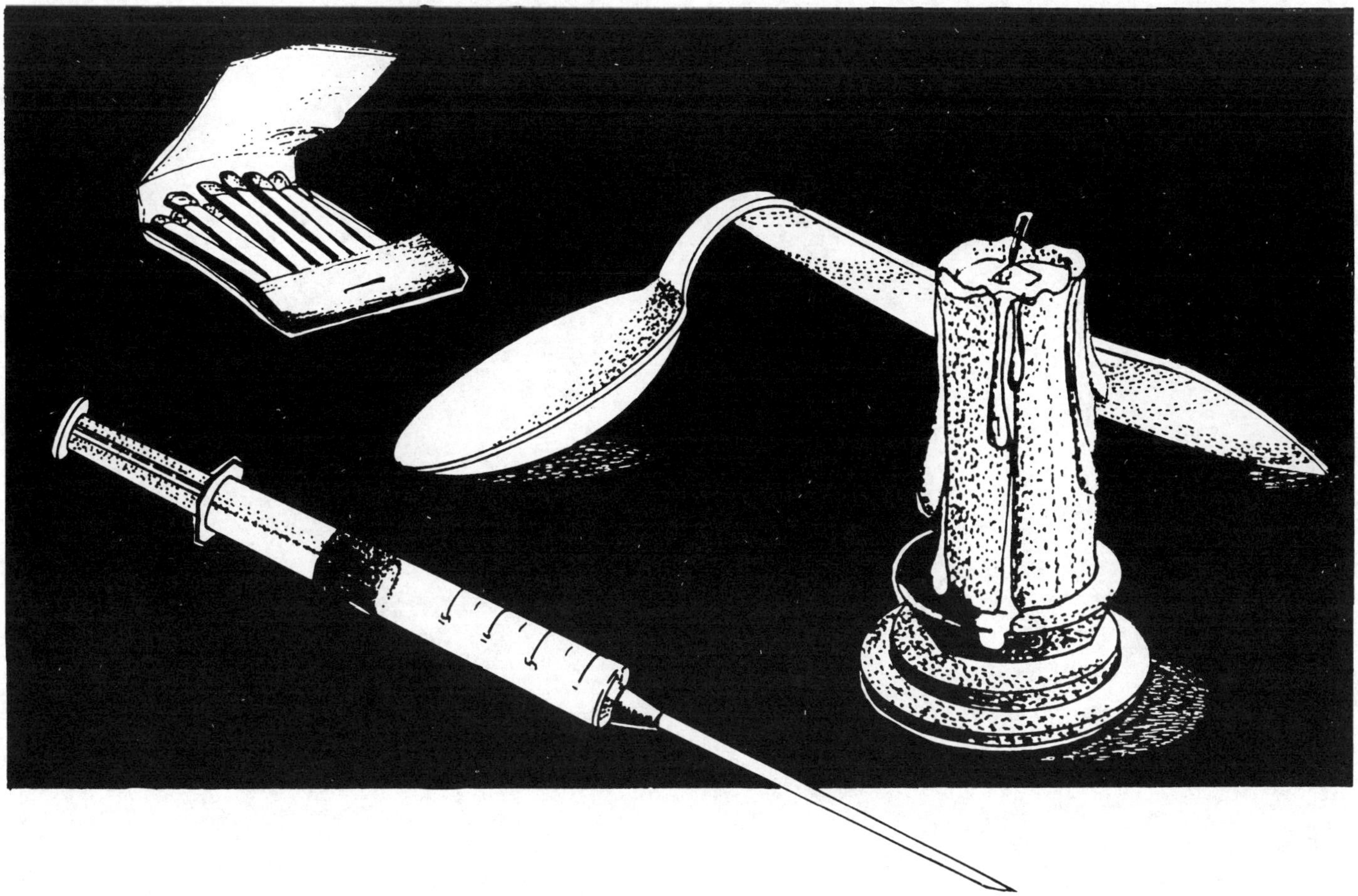

Unit Review - II.

✎ *Circle the correct answer . . .*

1 Barbiturates excite and stimulate the central nervous system, causing the drug user to feel alert.

A. True　　B. False

2 Barbiturates and minor tranquilizers produce an effect similar to . . .

A. Cocaine　　C. Alcohol
B. Marijuana　　D. LSD

3 Heroin is produced by chemically treating . . .

A. Barbiturates　　C. Morphine
B. Methadone　　D. Alcohol

4 The oldest drug known to man is . . .

A. Cocaine　　C. Heroin
B. Marijuana　　D. Alcohol

5 With some short acting barbiturates, withdrawal symptoms may not reach their peak for _______ after cessation of drug use.

A. 7 to 10 days　　C. One month
B. 21 days　　D. 24 to 48 months

6 Which one of the following does not belong in the opiate classification of drugs?

A. Methaqualone　　C. Codeine
B. Heroin　　D. Opium

7 Alcohol is considered a(n) . . .

A. Opiate　　C. Stimulant
B. Depressant　　D. Hallucinogen

8 Hypodermic needle users are subject to a host of infections. Shared needles are responsible for the spread of infections such as:

A. Cancer　　C. Hepatitis and AIDS
B. Flu　　D. Anemia and cystic fibrosis

Answers found on Page 203

Stimulants

Stimulants are a class of drugs capable of stimulating the central nervous system. They produce a feeling of increased alertness, euphoria and well being, decreased appetite, and an increased heart rate and blood pressure. Caffeine and nicotine are included in this class of drugs along with cocaine, amphetamines, and methamphetamine.

Stimulants

Drug Name	Street Name	What Does It Look Like?	Method of Use	What To Look For	Dangers and Harmful Effects
Cocaine	Coke, Toot, Snow, Nose Candy, Candy, Blow, Flake, White, Girl, C	White crystalline powder	Snorted (inhaled through nasal passages) Injected or Smoked	Small plastic bags or vials, or small squares of paper, personality changes, mood swings, depression, aggressive behavior	Physical and psychological dependence Malnutrition and physical deterioration Infection from needles Damage to nose and throat Damage to heart and lungs Coma or death from overdose Psychosis
Crack (Cocaine)	Rock, Crack Freebase	Beige or light brown pellets or white crystalline rocks	Smoked	Same as for Cocaine	Same as Cocaine with severe addiction
Amphetamines: Dexedrine Benzedrine Methedrine Biphetamine Desoxyns	Bennies, Black Beauties, Pink Hearts, White Cross, Whites, Crank, Speed, Pip Pills, Uppers, Wake Ups, Truck Drivers, Oklahoma Turn-arounds, Copilots, Beans, Black Mollies	Pills, Tablets, or Capsules, Liquid for injection	Taken orally, Injection, or Crushed and snorted (inhaled through nasal passage)	Changes in eating and sleeping patterns Increased energy Personality changes Mood swings Depression Aggressive behavior	Physical tolerance Psychological dependence Malnutrition and physical deterioration Damage to heart Psychosis, violent behavior Personality change Coma and death from overdose
Methamphetamines Methedrine	Crank, Crystal, Meth, Crystal Meth, Speed	Pills, White Powder, small rocks which resemble crystals	Taken orally, Snorted (inhaled through nasal passages)	Same as Amphetamines and Cocaine	Same as Amphetamines and Cocaine
ICE (Methamphetamines)	Ice, Rock, Freeze, Crystals, Glass	Small rocks which resemble crystals	Smoked	Same as Amphetamines and Cocaine	Same as Amphetamines with severe addiction

Cocaine

Historical Perspective **–** When Spanish explorers first landed in South America, they found the natives chewing on the leaves of a plant which energized the natives and provided them with refreshment. The plant was the Erythroxylon coca, a plant native to South America. The drug was used by the Incas of Peru and was restricted to the noble class. In 1860, a German scientist successfully extracted the alkaloid cocaine from the leaves of the plant. The use of cocaine increased with its inclusion in elixirs, cough syrups, and as a treatment for other common problems related to poor health. Though famous people, including Sigmund Freud, once touted its use, cocaine lost popularity in the late 1800's as physicians learned of its highly addictive properties. After the United States government placed controls on the possession and use of cocaine in 1914, use declined until the early 1970's when it skyrocketed again. Soon, the number of cocaine users tripled as the drug became known as a "recreational drug" that was relatively harmless. In the 1970's, users were satisfied with snorting it but the 1980's saw users beginning to smoke the drug in a volatile mixture. By the end of the 1980's, users had found a way to produce a highly concentrated smokeable form of the drug, called crack.

Origin **–** Cocaine is a natural stimulant derived from the leaves of the Erythroxylon coca plant. The Erythroxylon coca plant grows primarily in the upper Amazon basin and the Andean highlands. Cocaine, the main alkaloid derived from the coca leaves, is a powerful anesthetic and central nervous system stimulant.

Street Names **–** Coke, Toot, Snow, Nose Candy, Crack, Rock, Blow, Flake, Candy, White, Girl, C

Route of Administration **–** Cocaine is usually snorted (inhaled through the nasal passages) in doses of 15 to 50 mg. and is quickly absorbed through the mucus membranes of the nasal passages. The drug can also be liquefied and injected through hypodermic needles. Users have also perfected methods of smoking the drug by a chemical conversion process that produces a rock hard smokeable form of cocaine (crack) or by adding other chemicals (such as ether) to produce a highly volatile mixture (freebase) that can also be smoked.

Effects **–** Cocaine is a powerful anesthetic in eye and nose surgery, as well as in treatment of throat aliments, useful because it constricts the small blood vessels on the surface of a membrane, thus reducing bleeding.

Cocaine produces a number of physical changes in the user. It is a central nervous system stimulant that increases the heart rate, blood pressure and body temperature after ingestion. The user experiences a feeling of excitement, stimulation, and euphoria immediately after ingesting the drug. The feeling of excitement wears off after 5 to 10 minutes and the user is left feeling slightly depressed. After repeated use, the body begins to crave this feeling of excitement and stimulation to counteract the depressed feeling experienced after the drug wears off. Cocaine in even small doses has been shown to produce irregularities in heartbeat and blood pressure, and has led to heart attacks in relatively young and healthy users.

What To Look For – Look for small squares of paper or small plasic bags or vials with a white powder residue. The small square of paper measuring several inches is folded to make a leak proof pouch capable of holding a gram or less of cocaine. Cocaine users experience personality changes and may become suspicious and paranoid. They also experience dramatic and profound mood swings along with deep depression and suicidal thoughts and feelings. Cocaine causes the user to feel energized, often speaking rapidly or jumping from one topic of conversation to another. Users may become aggressive or violent while under the influence of cocaine, especially crack cocaine.

Long Term Effects – Repeated use of cocaine leads to malnutrition and physical deterioration. Snorting the drug damages the membrances of the nose and throat, while smoking the drug damages the throat and lungs. In low doses cocaine use damages the heart muscle by increasing the heart rate and blood pressure, while cutting off the flow of blood to the small vessels that feed the heart. This damage can occur in even first time or infrequent users of the drug.

Effects of Overdose – In high doses, cocaine can produce feelings of panic and paranoia. The user may be agitated and restless. As the level of the drug increases in the blood stream, heart rate and body temperature increase. At toxic levels, the user may experience visualizations that mimic hallucinations. When cocaine reaches life threatening proporations in the blood stream, the user experiences a loss of control over body functions. The user may have convulsions that range from mild seizures to convulsions capable of damaging the brain. Coma and death can occur as cocaine begins to overpower the vital functions of the body.

***Withdrawal Symptoms* –** Cocaine users experience both physical and psychological dependence. The user develops tolerance to the drug and goes through a withdrawal process (crash) upon cessation of use. The withdrawal syndrome lasts between 10 to 14 days and is characterized by: irritability, negativism, lack of energy, feelings of depression, sleepiness, fear, anxiety, paranoia, chills, nausea, vomiting, and may lead to a suicide attempt.

***Special Concerns* –** Cocaine, when sold on the street, is often cut with foreign substances to increase the volume. Milk sugar, lidocaine and procaine are among the most popular substances used to cut cocaine. PCP has also been found in cocaine purchased on the streets. Cocaine users cannot be sure of the quality or purity of the cocaine they purchase and thus run a serious personal risk when using this drug.

Amphetamines and Methamphetamines

Historical Perspective – Amphetamines were first synthesized in the late 1880's but did not become widely used until the 1930's to treat narcolepsy, which is a rare sleep disorder where the individual experiences an uncontrolled desire for sleep. Individuals with narcolepsy may fall asleep anywhere and at anytime. As amphetamines increased in popularity in medical practice, other uses for the drug were discovered. Use of the drug increased during World War II, when the drug was given to soldiers to increase alertness and overcome fatigue. Bomber pilots used the drug to stay awake on long bombing missions. After the war, popularity of the drug increased again as physicians began using the drug to treat obesity and depression. In the 1950's housewives and truck drivers joined the ranks of amphetamine users. During the 1960's, the abuse potential of the drug became evident.

In the early 1970's, the Federal government began to restrict and monitor the manufacture and distribution of amphetamines. At this time, the illicit manufacture and distribution of amphetamines on the black market increased. Currently, the manufacture of amphetamines is restricted and prescription of the drug is primarily limited to individuals requiring treatment for narcolepsy and for hyperactive behavior disorders in children. In the last few years, look alike drugs have become readily available on the black market. Tablets and capsules that look like true amphetamines, but may contain anything from caffeine and ephedrine compounds to amphetamine compounds, can be found on the black market.

Origin – Amphetamines and methamphetamines are so similar in composition and effect they produce that the only way to distinguish one from the other is by chemical analysis in the laboratory. Amphetamines, and its chemical cousin methamphetamines, are synthetic stimulant drugs manufactured for limited use in medicine for conditions of narcolepsy, hyperactive behavior disorders in children, and some forms of obsesity.

Street Names – Bennies, Black Beauties, Pink Hearts, White Cross, Whites, Crank, Crystal, Meth, Speed, Pep Pills, Uppers, Wake Ups, Truck Drivers, Oklahoma Turnarounds, Copilots, Beans, Black Mollies

Route of Administration **–** Amphetamines and methamphetamines are found in tablet, capsule, powder and liquid form. The most common route of administration for these drugs is by oral ingestion but they may also be snorted (inhaled nasally) in a powder form. The drug may also be smoked in a pipe or by spraying it on another smokeable substance (such as marijuana). The drug may be injected by placing it under the skin with a needle (skin popping) or may be injected directly into the vein (mainlining). Recently, a very potent smokeable form of methamphetamine (Ice) has been developed, with effects that last up to 12 hours.

Effects **–** Amphetamines and methamphetamine are central nervous system stimulants. The drugs create a feeling of energy and exhilaration, feelings of power and omnipotence, an increase in heart rate, blood pressure, and body temperature, and a loss of appetite. Hyperactive behavior may be a side effect. These drugs are also known to interfere with the body's ability to regulate temperature and the cardiovascular system. Effects of the drug may last anywhere from 2 to 12 hours depending on the type, amount, and potency taken.

What To Look For **–** Eating and sleeping patterns are disturbed with the drug user requiring fewer hours of sleep, along with a decreased appetite. Amphetamine and methamphetamine users show an increase in energy level and activity. Users may be over talkative with rapid speech and may change topics quickly. With continued use or with the use of large amounts, amphetamine and methamphetamine users may experience personality changes, suspiciousness or paranoia, with the potential for aggressive or violent behavior. Dramatic and profound mood swings or suicidal behavior may also be a sign of amphetamine or methamphetamine use.

Long Term Effects **–** Continued heavy use of amphetamines and methamphetamines leads to physical and emotional deterioration, as eating and sleeping patterns are disrupted. Long term heavy use of amphetamines and methamphetamines can lead to personality changes which include psychotic thinking and behavior that resembles paranoid schizophrenia. Visual and auditory hallucinations are a characteristic of psychotic thinking. Amphetamine and methamphetamine abusers become unpredictable and may become physically aggressive and violent.

Effects of Overdose **–** Amphetamine and methamphetamine overdose is characterized by marked impairment in decision making ability and poor judgment, increased suspiciousness and paranoia, along with an interruption of eating and sleeping patterns. Agitation, vomiting, flushed skin, tremors, abdominal cramps, dizziness, flushed skin, chest pains, and sweating are symptoms of toxic levels of amphetamine and methamphetamine. In high doses, amphetamines and methamphetamines may lead to cardiac arrest as the heart becomes overstimulated which may lead to coma and death.

Withdrawal Symptoms – Research shows that stimulant drug users develop a psychological dependence to the euphoric and powerful feelings produced by use of the drug. There is much controversy concerning the development of physical dependence on the drug. Heavy amphetamine and methamphetamine users experience profound depression after the cessation of use of the drug. Apathy, fatigue, and disturbed sleep accompany this state of emotional depression. Withdrawal may also include agitation, confusion or disorientation, anxiety, or a fear of dying. Acute withdrawal symptoms may last for several days. Personality changes, feelings of depression and anxiety accompanied by suicidal thinking may persist for several months after the drug user stops taking the drug.

Unit Review - III.

✎ *Circle the correct answer . . .*

❶ Cocaine is a powerful anesthetic drug that leaves the user feeling very sedated, quiet, and lethargic.

A. True B. False

❷ Amphetamines were given to soldiers during World War II to increase their alertness and reduce fatigue.

A. True B. False

❸ The United States government placed controls on the posession and use of cocaine in . . .

A. 1934 C. 1970
B. 1917 D. 1914

❹ "Ice" is considered to be . . .

A. Cocaine C. Barbiturates
B. Methamphetamine D. Frozen water you put in a drink

❺ Long term heavy use of amphetamines and methamphetamines can lead to personality changes, psychotic thinking, and behavior that resembles . . .

A. Lethargy C. A conduct disorder
B. Depression D. Paranoid schizophrenia

❻ With amphetamines and methamphetamine, personality changes, feelings of depression and anxiety, accompanied by suicidal thinking may persist for ____________ after the drug user stops taking the drug.

A. 2 to 3 days C. Several months
B. 10 to 14 days D. 21 to 25 days

❼ The feeling of excitement and stimulation produced by cocaine usually wears off in about . . .

A. 20 to 25 minutes C. 30 minutes
B. 5 to 10 minutes D. One hour

❽ Cocaine is a safe recreational drug that does not have addictive qualities.

A. True B. False

Answers found on Page 203

Hallucinogens

Hallucinogens (or psychedelics) are a class of drugs capable of changing emotions, thinking, sensation, and feelings of self-awareness in the user. Along with these changes in perception, the user may experience illusions and/or hallucinations along with a break with reality.

Hallucinogens

Drug Name	Street Name	What Does It Look Like?	Method of Use	What To Look For	Dangers and Harmful Effects
Marijuana THC Hashish Hash Oil	Herb, Pot, Grass, Weed, Reefer, Simsemilia, Skunk, Dirt Weed, Homegrown, Dope, Red, Panama Red, Columbians, Hawaiian, Jamaican, Oil	Dried parsley mixed with seeds and stems. Soft gelatin capsules Brown or black cakes or balls of tar Concentrated syrupy liquid	Most often smoked, may be taken orally in capsule form, may be made into tea or baked in brownies.	Sweet burnt odor. Pipes, roach clips, cigarette rolling papers, apathetic or amotivational behavior.	Impaired perception and memory, poor concentration, decreased alertness, and an inability to perform complicated tasks. Possible damage to lungs, heart and reproductive system. Psychological dependence
Lysergic Acid Diethylamide (LSD)	Acid, Vitamin A, Blotter, Window Pane, Purple Haze, Blue Devil, Cubes, Microdot, Green or Red Dragon, Laughing Clowns	Brightly colored tablets Clear liquid Thin squares of gelatin Impregnated blotter paper	Most often taken orally, may be injected, gelatin and liquid form may be placed in the eyes	Dilated pupils Mood swings Uncontrolled laughter Illusions and/or hallucinations Impaired thinking and judgment	Irritability and irrational thinking and behavior, paranoia, loss of touch with reality, emotional breakdown, insomnia and restlessness, flashbacks and panic attacks.
Psilocybin	Magic Mushrooms, Mushrooms, Shrooms	Fresh, frozen, or dried mushrooms	Mushrooms may be taken orally by chewing and swallowing, made into tea, or may be smoked	Dilated pupils Mood swings Illusions and/or hallucinations Impaired thinking and judgment	Anxiety, restlessness, insomnia, irritability, loss of touch with reality, impaired memory and perception
Peyote and Mescaline	Cactus, Buttons, Mesc	Hard brown discs Tablets Capsules	Buttons may be taken orally by chewing or swallowing or in tea, also may be smoked. Tablets or capsules taken orally	Dilated pupils Mood swings Illusions and/or hallucinations Impaired thinking and judgment	Anxiety, restlessness, insomnia, loss of touch with reality, emotional breakdown, impaired memory and perception
Phencyclidine (PCP)	Angel Dust, Dust, Killer Weed, Hog, Lovely, Loveboat, DOA (Dead on Arrival)	White crystalline powder Liquid Capsules Tablets	PCP may be taken orally, injected, smoked, or snorted (inhaled)	Dreamlike state, confusion, sense of dying, paranoia, assaultive behavior, slurred speech, blurred vision, uncoordination	Memory loss, inability to concentrate, insomnia, chronic or recurrent psychosis, withdrawal may produce short to long term depression. Death from accidents. Death from overdose.

Cannabis Sativa is the scientific name for marijuana. The resin produced by the plant contains the active ingredient THC (Tetrahydracannabinol). The leaves or flower buds of the plant are dryed and crushed before being smoked or eaten to produce a high.

Marijuana

***Historical Perspective* –** Around for centuries, there is evidence to suggest that marijuana was raised for its medicinal qualities by the Chinese as early as the third century B.C. In the ancient Middle East, Asia, and Africa, hemp was grown for its use in religious ceremonies. In the United States, its use as a psychoactive drug began in the 1800's. In the 19th century, it was prescribed as a pain reliever, anticonvulsant, sleep aid and muscle relaxant. Hemp was used extensively in the making of rope before World War II until the development of synthetic fibers, when it was no longer needed. In the 1920's and 1930's, myths spread concerning the connection between marijuana use and violent behavior, and physical and mental illness. Law enforcement agencies erroneously tied marijuana to crime. In 1937, the Marijuana Tax act was passed which made the use of marijuana illegal for any purpose. Its use spread slowly until the student movement of the sixties when Marijuana became a symbol of rebellion and personal freedom. By the late sixties, the battle cry was "Make marijuana legal" and individual states were called upon to decide the legal sanctions against its possession and use. Penalties for Marijuana use today vary from state to state and range from a misdemeanor to a felony.

***Origin* –** Marijuana comes from the Cannabis Sativa hemp plant which was used primarily for making rope before the invention of synthetic fibers. The plant can grow to heights of 12 to 14 feet and as it matures, produces a sticky resin that covers its leaves and flower buds. This resin produced by the plant contains its active ingredient, THC (Tetrahydracannabinol). Marijuana is classified as a mild hallucinogen, grows wild as a weed in many regions of the world but does best in a semi-tropical environment.

***Street Names* –** Pot, Grass, Herb, Reefer, Weed, Columbian, Hawaiian, Jamacian, Sinsemilia, Skunk, Ditch Weed, Dirt Weed, Panama Red, Red, Purple Hair, Dope, Mary Jane, Smoke, Stick, Tea, J, Jay, Hemp

***Route of Administration* –** Smoking marijuana is the most popular means of ingestion. The leaves or flower buds are dryed, crushed and the seeds and stems discarded. The flower buds are the most sought after because they contain the highest concentration of plant resin containing THC. The leaves or the buds are smoked or eaten to produce the high.

ZIG-ZAG
Bambú
1.5
Cigarette Paper
ZIG-ZAG

Effects – The effects of the drug THC vary with each individual. Upon ingesting the drug, THC is rapidly absorbed through the lungs and passes into the blood stream. THC is absorbed into most tissues of the body, including the brain, the heart, and fatty tissues. In most people, THC produces a mild euphoria, a feeling of reduced inhibitions and relaxation, a preoccupation with sights and sounds, time distortion, and disoriented behavior. There is some evidence to suggest that smoking marijuana produces an increased appetite called the "munchies".

An individual begins to experience the effects of the drug approximately 3 to 5 minutes after ingestion. The effects last 2 to 4 hours depending on the strength and amount consumed. The short term effects of the drug are red eyes, a slight dilation of the pupils, increased blood pressure and heart rate, mild tremors, anxiety, paranoia, and a dry mouth.

What To Look For – When marijuana is burned, it has a strong distinctive sweet odor that resembles that of burning alfalfa or rope. The odor hangs in the air and permeates the user's clothing and hair. While under the influence, the user may appear animated and excited, followed by lethargic and apathetic behavior. The user may experience periods of random laughter. Pupils may be dilated and eyes may appear bloodshot. The user may also experience distortions of perception and hallucinations. Empty plastic bags with green flakey residue, cigarette rolling papers, pipes and bongs are indicators of marijuana use.

Long Term Harmful Effects – In large doses, marijuana can produce feelings of strangeness and unreality, as well as depersonalization, feelings of fear, panic, and impending death. In higher doses, marijuana can produce delusions and hallucinations.

Withdrawal Symptoms – There is no clear evidence which demonstrates that marijuana users develop physical tolerance to the drug and experience withdrawal symptoms. There are indications that chronic users experience a decreased appetite, insomnia, and hyperactivity upon cessation of drug use.

A Bong is a water pipe used for smoking marijuana, hashish, or cocaine. The pipe is designed to concentrate the smoke allowing the user to get a quick, intense high.

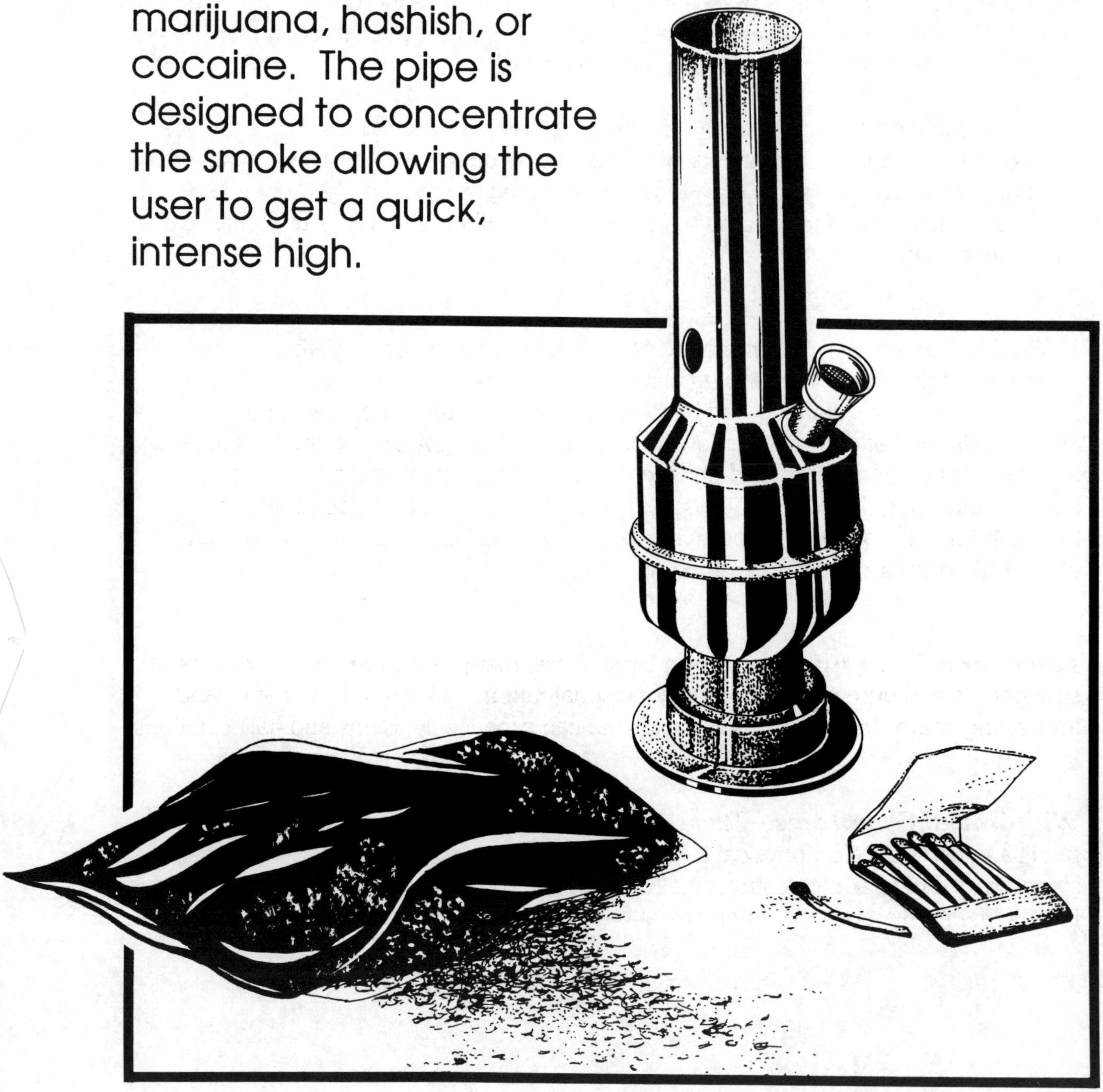

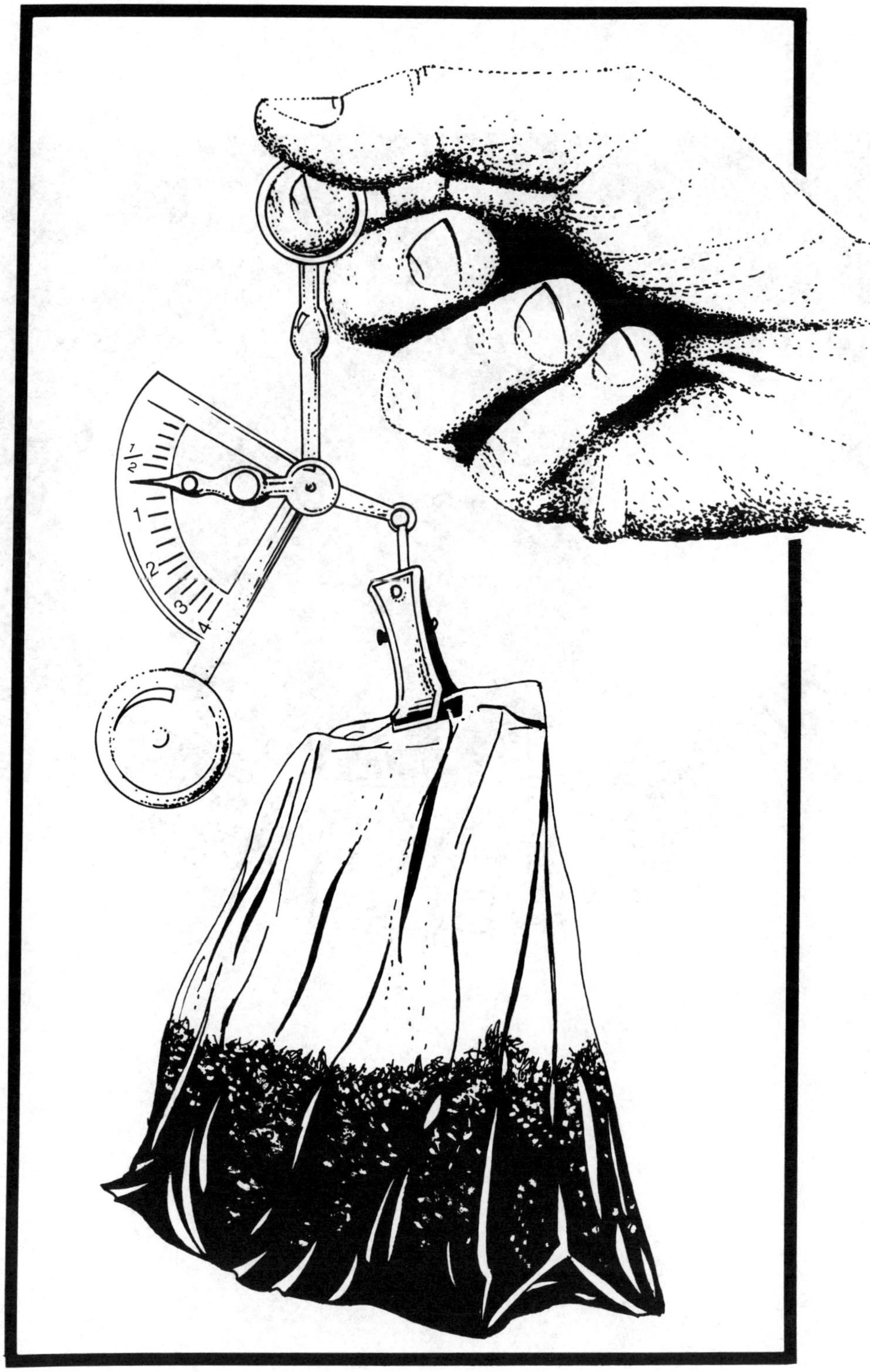

1/2
1
2
3
4

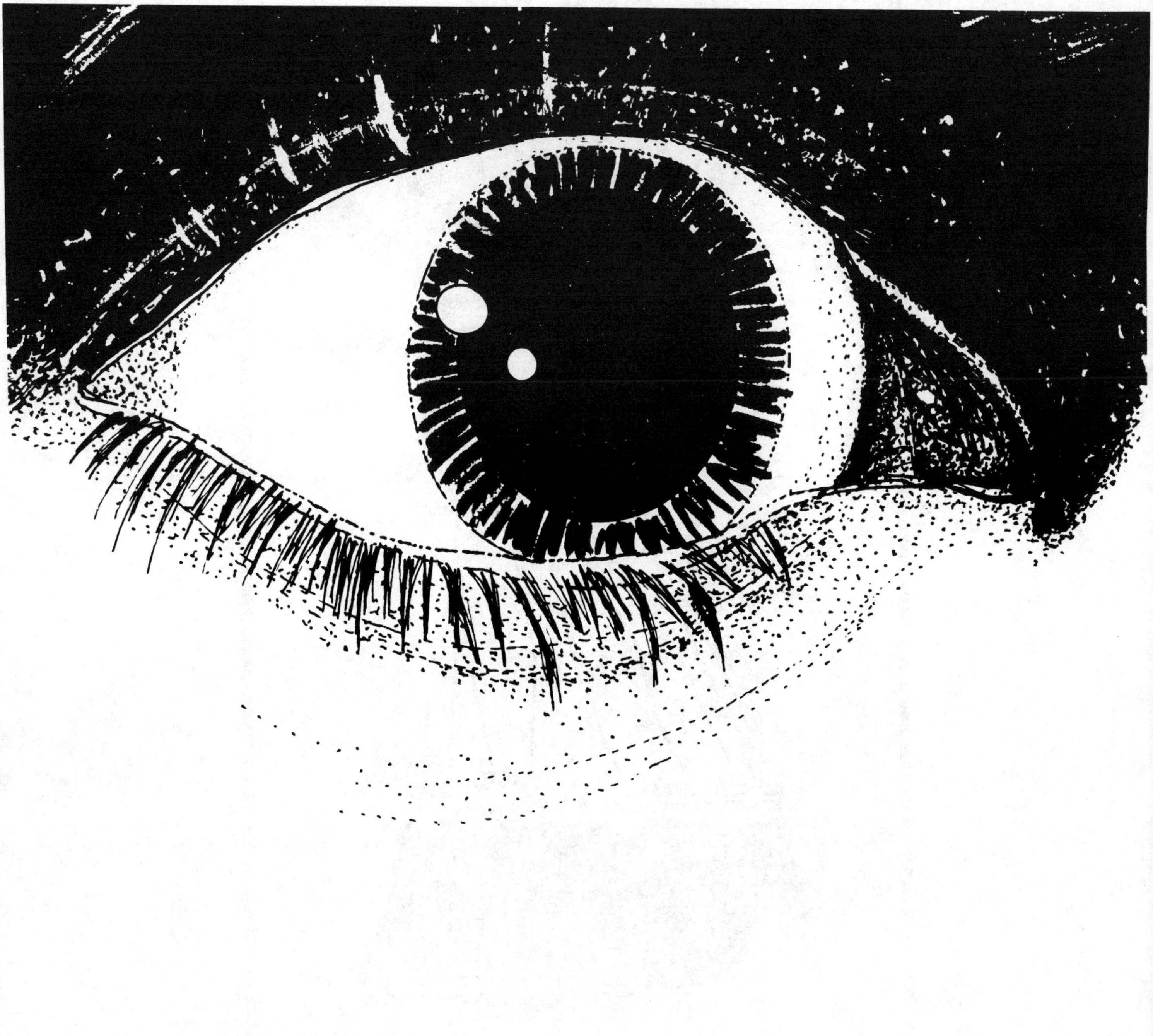

LSD
D-Lysergic Acid Diethylamide

Historical Perspective **–** D-Lysergic acid diethylamide or LSD was first synthesized in 1938 and its hallucinogenic properties discovered quite by accident. In 1938, Swiss chemist Albert Hofmann was working with the chemical when some of the substance was absorbed through his skin. He experienced dramatic visualizations and hallucinations. During the 1950's, the United States government conducted research using LSD on soldiers to determine its usefulness as a chemical weapon in times of war. By the 1960's, LSD made its way into the counter culture movement in the United States. The use of LSD was promoted by notable scientists such as Dr. Timothy Leary and viewed as a drug that could help the user with 'mind expansion' and creativity leading to a total cosmic awareness. LSD could be used legally in the United States until 1968.

Origin **–** LSD is synthesized in the laboratory from a fungus called ergot. This fungus is common to wheat and rye grains as well as sunflowers.

Street Names **–** Acid, Laughing Clowns, Clowns, Vitamin A, Window Pane, Purple Haze, Haze, California Sunshine, Sunshine, Blotter, Blue Devil, White Lightening, Woodstock

Route of Administration **–** The most common method of ingestion is orally. The drug may also be injected and the gelatin and liquid forms of the drug can be placed in the eye. Oral administration effects the user within 30 to 45 minutes, injection within 5 to 10 minutes. The average 'trip' lasts anywhere from 8 to 12 hours.

LSD is one of the most potent drugs known, so potent that doses are measured in micrograms. A dose of 25 micrograms of LSD is enough to produce changes within the average person. A dose of 100 micrograms is considered an average dose. Even a small variation in the size of the dose may produce a large variation in effects.

Effects – LSD produces bodily changes: an increased heart rate, a rise in blood prssure, increased body temperature, pupil dilation, tremors, sweaty palms, chills, nausea, and a lack of appetite. The psychological effects vary depending on the size of the dose, the mood and attitude of the user, and the environment in which the drug is ingested. LSD produces illusions and/or hallucinations, changes in the perception of sight, hearing, taste, time, space, and body image. The user may experience colors as being more intense and vivid, or colors may change and melt together. The user may also experience objects as free flowing and not fixed, leading to the perception that objects are alive and part of a living breathing world.

What To Look For – The LSD user may emit a strong body odor and appear restless and agitated. If you find small ampules with a clear liquid, blotter paper with what will look like small water spots, tablets or capsules of various colors, then your adolescent may be using LSD. Also, the user may exhibit signs of hallucinations, feelings of detachment, mood swings, incoherent speech, cold sweaty hands and feet, vomiting, laughing or crying. The user may also appear suicidal or homicidal.

Long Term Harmful Effects – There is a great deal of controversy in the scientific world as to the long term hazards of LSD use, including 'flashbacks'. Flashbacks are a reoccurrence of the psychological state of the drug taking experience. The LSD user feels that he/she is re-experiencing the 'trip' without having taken the drug. This is a frightening experience. Scientists are also worried about the possibility that LSD can bring on psychosis for the user who is prone to mental illness, is psychologically unstable, or who is unprepared for the intensity of the drug experience.

Effects of Overdose – An overdose of LSD can mean a more intense and longer 'trip'. In high doses, the user may experience feelings of panic and anxiety, depersonalization, paranoia, fear of dying, psychosis, and possible injury or death due to accidents.

Withdrawal Symptoms – Research has not shown that LSD users develop a physical dependence to the drug or experience withdrawal symptoms as a result of prolonged drug use. Users do develop a tolerance to the drug that may dramatically diminish the effects they experience and may experience a psychological dependence to the drug.

Psilocybe Mushrooms

Historical Perspective – Psilocybin has its roots in the religious ceremonies of the Aztecs. Ample archaeological evidence supports the fact that hallucinogenic mushrooms were used in the Aztec temples by the high priest or shaman. Each variety of mushroom held a special place in the day to day religious practices of the temple. These sacred mushrooms survived in religious traditions for hundreds of years. Unlike Peyote, there is little evidence to suggest that the hallucinogenic mushroom was used by the tribes of North America. The use of the mushroom was introduced into the United States from Mexico in recent times and gained popularity during the late sixties and early seventies.

Origin – Psilocybin is a hallucinogen that is found in ninety varieties of mushrooms native to Europe, as well as North and Central America. It produces hallucinations and psychedelic effects much like that of LSD.

Street Names – Magic Mushrooms, Shrooms, Buttons

Route of Administration – Mushrooms upon harvest are processed by slicing the mushroom and freezing, or drying in a dehydrator. Psilocybe mushrooms which produce the greatest effects are often processed by a freeze drying method. Once processed, the mushroom can be ingested orally, by chewing and swallowing the mushroom or it may be brewed into a tea. Dried mushrooms may also be smoked in a pipe. Usual doses of 5 to 10 grams of dried mushroom produce effects similar to a mild form of LSD. Average length of a 'trip' is 4 to 6 hours.

Effects – The effects of psilocybin are similar to that of LSD. Initially, the drug produces increased heart rate, a rise in blood pressure, pupil dilation, tremors, chills, nausea, and a lack of appetite. The psychological effects vary depending on the size of the dose taken. Psilocybe produces illusions and/or hallucinations, changes in the perception of sight, hearing, taste, time, space, and body image.

What To Look For – The user may exhibit signs of hallucinations, feelings of detachment, mood swings, incoherent speech, cold sweaty hands and feet, vomiting, laughing, or crying. The person may also appear anxious or paranoid, as well as suicidal or homicidal.

Long Term Harmful Effects – As with LSD, there is a great deal of controversy in the scientific world as to the long term hazards of Psilocybin use. The most pronounced symptoms of long term use are anxiety, paranoia, restlessness, and irritability. The drug user runs the risk of experiencing memory and perceptual impairments, emotional breakdown, and loss of touch with reality.

Effects of Overdose – Large doses of psilocybin will exaggerate both the duration and intensity of effects. The user may feel emotionally uncomfortable, experience anxiety attacks, tremors, nausea, and vomiting.

Withdrawal Symptoms – There is no scientific evidence to support the contention that psilocybin users develop a tolerance to the drug, although it is suggested in the literature that users experience diminished effects after repeated use. Psilocybin users report irritability, restlessness and fatigue the day after cessation of drug use.

Peyote

Historical Perspective – Peyote is another hallucinogen that can be traced back to the religious alter of the Aztec high priests. The drug was considered a divine substance. The term Mescaline refers to the drug peyote. The name Mescaline evolved because of its use by a band of Indians called the Mescalero Apaches. Historians credit the Mescalero Apaches with the spread of peyote to other tribes of North America. Peyote became an integral part of the religious practices of several bands of North American Indians. In modern times, the use of peyote for religious purposes is documented in the teachings of the Native American Church and was protected under the freedom of religion statutes until just recently when the Supreme Court ruled its use illegal.

Origin – Peyote is derived from the peyote cactus which grows in the desert southwest of the United States and Mexico. The spineless greyish-brown colored cactus grows to a height of only three inches above the ground. The cactus top is sliced into sections and dried. These dried sections called 'buttons' can be consumed later. Mescaline, the active alkaloid dervied from the cactus, is a white crystalline powder that is synthesized in the laboratory. Because of its purity and potency, Mescaline is the preferred form of the drug.

Street Names – Buttons, Cactus, Mesc

Route of Administration – Peyote buttons are chewed and swallowed in dry form, made into tea, or placed in milk or coffee. Because the peyote button has a strong foul taste, users often prefer to dissolve it in coffee or milk to neutralize the taste. Mescaline can be found in a crystalline form which can be swallowed in tablet or capsule form, or dissolved in liquid. This form of the drug is more agreeable to the user.

Approximately 500 milligrams is an average dose with effects lasting for 4 to 12 hours. After ingesting the drug, the user experiences its effects in 1 to 3 hours.

Effects – The drug produces many of the same effects as LSD: an increased heart rate, a rise in blood pressure, pupil dilation, tremors, nausea, vomiting, and lack of appetite. The psychological effects vary depending on the size of the dose taken. Peyote produces the same type of illusions and/or hallucinations as does LSD, producing changes in the perception of sight, hearing, taste, time, space, and body image.

What To Look For – The peyote user may appear restless and agitated, exhibit signs of hallucinations, feelings of detachment, mood swings, incoherent speech, loss of coordination, nausea, vomiting, inappropriate laughing, or crying. The user may also appear anxious or paranoid, as well as suicidal or homicidal.

Long Term Harmful Effects – Along with LSD and Psilocybin, there is a great deal of controversy in the scientific world as to the long term hazards of Peyote use. Symptoms of long term Peyote use are the same as with the other members of the hallucinogen family and include anxiety, paranoia, restlessness, and irritability. The user runs the risk of memory and perceptual impairments, emotional breakdown, and loss of touch with reality.

Effects of Overdose – As with the other hallucinogens, large doses of Peyote will exaggerate the effects of lower doses and increase the duration and intensity of the experience. Along with this, the Peyote user may feel emotionally uncomfortable, may experience anxiety attacks, tremors, nausea, and vomiting. In high doses, Peyote can have toxic effects, can negatively impact the digestive system and in high doses may be fatal.

Withdrawal Symptoms – As with Psilocybin, there is no scientific evidence to support the contention that Peyote users develop a tolerance to the drug. Peyote users report irritability, restlessness and fatigue the day after cessation of drug use.

Peyote is derived from the Peyote cactus which grows in the desert southwest of the United States and Mexico. The spineless greyish-brown colored cactus grows to a height of only three inches. The cactus top is sliced into sections and dried.

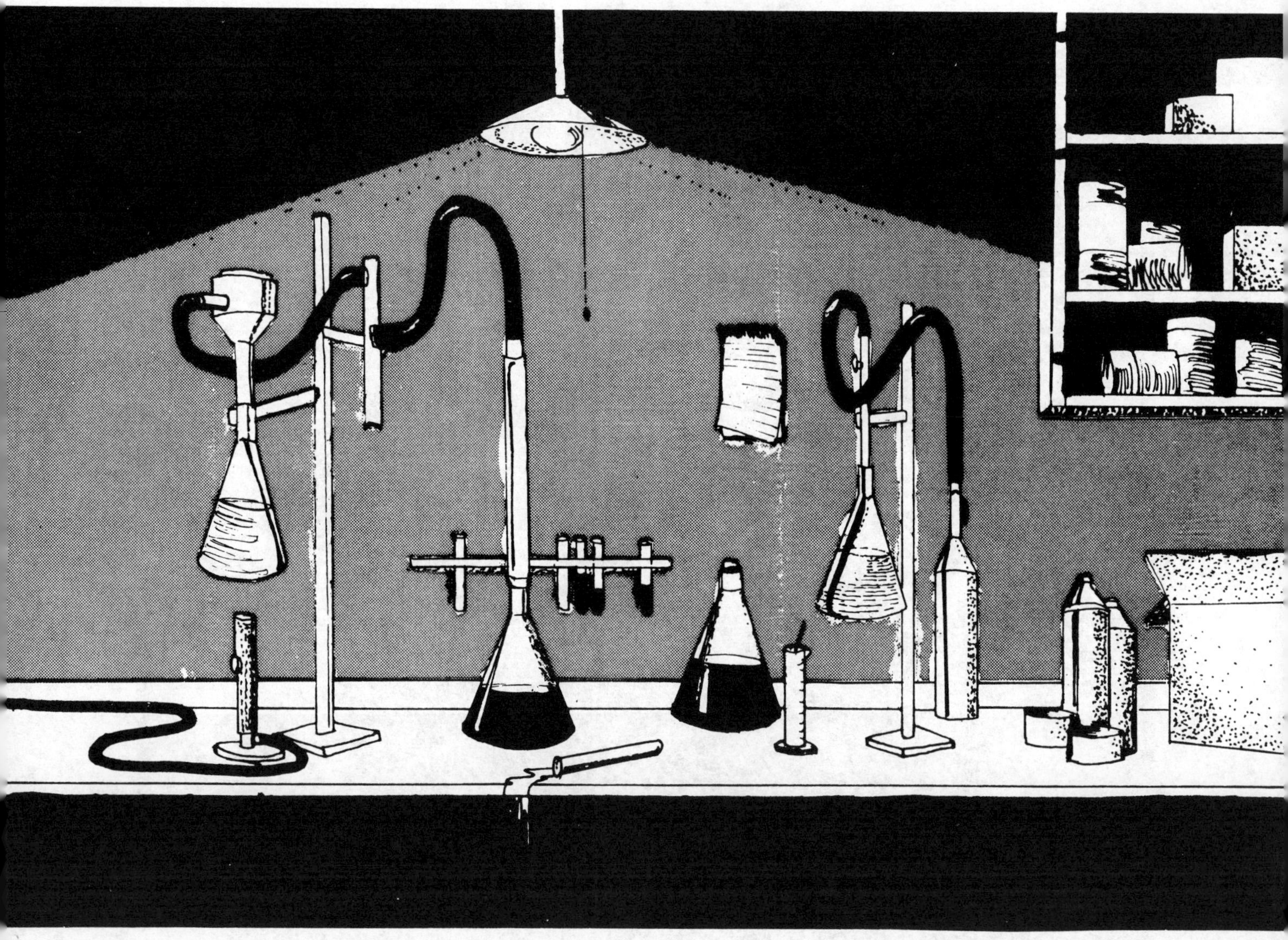

PCP

PCP (Phencyclidine) is better known as angel dust. A non-narcotic anesthetic agent that can produce serious adverse behavioral reactions, PCP produces a number of different effects on the user and, because it lacks a clear distinction, is classified as a member of the hallucinogen family.

Historical Perspective **–** Phencyclidine was originally used in an experimental form in the 1950's as a human anesthetic. Use of the drug in medicine indicated that the drug was unsafe for human use. Patients experienced side effects ranging from confusion and delirium, to violent behavioral reactions. The drug was legally manufactured in the 1960's for use in veterinary medicine. In 1978, the manufacturer of the drug stopped production. Phencyclidine found on the market today is produced in clandestine laboratories. Because the chemicals to make PCP are easy to obtain and the formula is easy to duplicate, drug dealers can obtain huge profits from its manufacture and distribution.

Origin **–** PCP (Phencyclidine) is a synthetic drug manufactured in the laboratory. In its pure form, PCP is a white crystalline powder. Because of poor quality control in its illegal manufacture, its color can range from tan to brown, and its consistency from powder to a gummy mass.

Street Names **–** Angel Dust, Dust, Hog, Super Hog, Peace Pill, Killer Weed, Embalming Fluid, Rocket Fuel

Route of Administration **–** PCP may be taken orally, injected, snorted (inhaled nasally), or smoked. It comes in tablet, capsule, powder, and liquid form. The most common form of ingestion is to spray the drug on a leafy material such as marijuana and smoke it. It is also smoked on oregano, parsley, and mint.

Effects **–** The effects of PCP on the user are unpredictable. A moderate amount of the drug can produce feelings of alienation, depersonalization, detachment, and estrangement from the surrounding environment. The drug also produces feelings of numbness, impaired memory, coordination and slurred or blocked speech. The person using PCP may experience auditory and visual hallucinations, distorted images including body image distortion, severe mood disorders, anxiety and feelings of impending doom. Because PCP is an anesthetic compound, it produces a feeling of numbness, an inability to feel pain, which can lead to serious injury.

What To Look For – The most easily recognized symptoms of PCP use include anxiety and restlessness, paranoia, a blank stare, rapid and involuntary eye movements, and an exaggerated gait. The user may become easily angered and demonstrate increased strength, aggressiveness, and violent hostility.

Long Term Effects – Long term use of PCP leads to impaired memory, speech, coordination, judgment, and disorientation. PCP users risk extreme psychological reactions, although it must be noted that casual or one time use can produce the same extreme personality and emotional changes. PCP is one of the few drugs that can bring on psychosis similar to schizophrenia. Drug induced psychosis can last for long periods of time and can occur long after the drug has left the body.

Effects of Overdose – Large doses of PCP lead to increased heart rate and blood pressure, loss of body control, loss of feeling, an increased pain threshold, rapid eye movement, sweating, and violent behavioral reactions. PCP users are unpredictable and at high risk of injuring themselves and others. PCP overdose victims risk convulsions, coma, and death related to heart and lung failure.

Withdrawal Symptoms – PCP leaves the body at a slow rate, is stored in the fatty tissue of the body for long periods of time and can be reabsorbed. This may lead to unpredictable behavior for some time after discontinuing use. PCP causes feelings of mental depression which become more pronounced upon cessation of drug use. There is some evidence that PCP users develop an increased tolerance to the drug.

Unit Review - IV.

Circle the correct answer . . .

1. Which is the most potent mind altering drug known to man?

   A. PCP
   B. Alcohol
   C. Marijuana
   D. LSD

2. The active ingredient in marijuana that makes the user feel high is . . .

   A. PCP
   B. MTV
   C. THC
   D. LSD

3. Psilocybin has its roots in the religious ceremonies of Aztecs.

   A. True
   B. False

4. Marijuana when burned has a strong sweet odor which resembles . . .

   A. Burnt roses
   B. Burnt rope or alfalfa
   C. Burnt toast
   D. Burnt dog hair

5. Mescaline is derived from the Mexican cactus . . .

   A. Peyote cactus
   B. Barrel cactus
   C. Sequoia cactus
   D. Sorrel cactus

6. Marijuana users begin to experience the effects of the drug approximately _______________ after smoking the drug.

   A. One hour
   B. 20 minutes
   C. 1/2 hour
   D. 3 to 5 minutes

7. The effects of PCP on the user and even casual or one time use can lead to . . .

   A. Violent psychotic reactions
   B. A good night's sleep
   C. No noticeable effects
   D. Unending bliss

Answers found on Page 203

Inhalants

Inhalants are a class of drugs that are capable of producing intoxication, euphoria, and feelings of well-being. Inhalants are any chemical substance that gives off vapors or fumes which can be inhaled to produce intoxication. Many commercial cleaning products, as well as automotive additives and gases, produce vapors that can be inhaled.

Inhalants

<table>
<tr><th>Drug Name</th><th>Street Name</th><th>What Does It Look Like?</th><th>Method of Use</th><th>What To Look For</th><th>Dangers and Harmful Effects</th></tr>
<tr><td>Hydrocarbons</td><td>Solvents</td><td>Cans of aerosol propellants, glue, gasoline, paint thinner</td><td>Vapors inhaled</td><td rowspan="6">Flecks of paint or other substances around nose or mouth
Stains or chemical damage to clothes
Red marks, burns, or blisters around nose or mouth
Rags, pop cans, plastic bags, or paper bags which contain a chemical substance or chemical smell
Chemical smell on breath or bad breath.</td><td rowspan="6">Serious physical and emotional effects which include:
Liver and kidney damage
Depressed immunity to infections
Weight loss
Memory impairment
Fatigue
Irritability, agitation
Hostility and aggression
Bizarre behavior
Cardiac arrhythmias
Emotional depression
Psychosis
Coma
Death</td></tr>
<tr><td>Chlorohydrocarbons</td><td>Aerosol sprays</td><td>Aerosol paint cans
Containers of cleaning fluids</td><td>Vapors inhaled</td></tr>
<tr><td>Nitrous Oxide</td><td>Laughing Gas</td><td>Propellant in aerosol cans
Dental gas</td><td>Vapors inhaled</td></tr>
<tr><td>Amyl Nitrate</td><td>Poppers, Snappers</td><td>Yellow liquid in ampules</td><td>Vapors inhaled</td></tr>
<tr><td>Butyl Nitrate</td><td>Rush, Locker Room</td><td>Bottles of liquid</td><td>Vapors inhaled</td></tr>
<tr><td></td><td></td><td></td><td></td></tr>
</table>

KEEP THIS
CHILDREN AND SMALL CHILDREN
WARNING: TOXIC

Inhalants

Historical Perspective – Consciousness altering inhalants can be traced back to the beginning of recorded history. The ancient Hebrews inhaled the vapors of burning spices as part of their religious practice. The Greeks inhaled cold gases to alter their state of consciousness. For centuries, the religious ceremonies of the South American natives have included hallucinogenic snuff preparations. The abuse of industrial chemical preparations has escalated over the last thirty years with the development of new chemical technologies. Inhalant abuse became a serious concern when glue sniffing was identified as an adolescent problem.

The average age range of inhalant abusers is 7 to 17, with the average abuser being $12^1/_2$ years of age. Studies show that more boys than girls abuse inhalants, although girls are starting to catch up.

Origin – Inhalants are any chemical substances that give off vapors or fumes that can be inhaled to produce a feeling of euphoria. The most common inhalants are commercially produced solvents and cleaning agents.

Street Names – Huff, Rush, Locker Room, Snappers, Poppers, Laughing Gas

Route of Administration – The chemical substance is usually placed in a bag or other container to concentrate the vapors or fumes for inhalation. The vapors or fumes are inhaled and enter the lungs where the chemical is distributed into the bloodstream. The chemicals contained in the vapors move quickly through the bloodstream and cross the blood/brain barrier and enter the brain. Many of the chemical vapors work directly on the central nervous system and depress heart rate and blood pressure. The high produced by inhalants is short lived with a duration of one minute to one hour depending on the chemical substance used.

Effects – The effects of many of these commercially produced chemical agents is similar to that of alcohol. The user feels a sense of euphoria and well being, decreased inhibitions, slurred speech, a loss of coordination, bad breath, nausea, nose bleeds, and coughing.

Inhalant users may also experience muscle spasms, cardiac arrhythmias, double vision, ringing in the ears, and hallucinations. Inhalants may alter the perceptions of the abuser leading to delusions, hallucinations and an altered perception of reality. The effect of inhalants on behavior is unpredictable and can lead to serious injury or death.

There are several chemical agents in the inhalant category that are commercially produced as drugs. Nitrous Oxide (laughing gas) used as an anesthetic, can provide a fatal outcome as the drug replaces oxygen in the system and causes the user to die of anoxia.

Amyl Nitrate is a drug used for heart patients because it dilates the blood vessels and makes the heart beat faster. Butyl Nitrate sold in record stores under the name 'Rush' or 'Locker Room' produces a high that lasts from a few seconds to a couple of minutes. Butyl Nitrate also produces decreased blood pressure, increased heart rate, dizziness, and commonly headaches.

What To Look For – Parents should look for discarded rags or chemical containers that are hidden or out of place. Rags, pop cans, plastic bags, and paper bags which contain a chemical substance or have a strong chemical smell are signs of inhalant abuse. Look for a strange smell on your adolescent's breath and clothing as well as spills on clothing, as many of the chemicals abused as inhalants may stain or damage clothing material. At times, inhalant abusing adolescents will have flecks of paint or other substances or chemical burns appearing as red marks and blisters around their nose and mouth.

Long Term Effects – Inhalant abusers run the risk of serious physical and emotional problems as a result of long term use, including liver and kidney damage, brain damage, depressed immunity from infections, and weight loss. Along with these are problems with memory impairment, fatigue, irritability, agitation, and hostility. Studies indicate that the use of certain inhalants (i.e. gas) reduces I.Q. scores in adolescents, as well as produces personality changes. Scientists have not yet concluded that these changes are permanent.

Effects of Overdose – The chemical agents abused as inhalants are volatile substances that can produce violent and fatal reactions in the user. Inhalant abusers experience bizarre behavior, cardiac arrhythmias, emotional depression, psychosis, coma, and death.

Withdrawal Symptoms – The use of these chemicals can lead to psychological dependence. Also, the abuse of certain inhalants may lead to an increased tolerance to the chemical substance, as well as withdrawal symptoms. Commonly reported withdrawal symptoms include headache, chills, abdominal pain, muscular cramps, tremors, and hallucinations.

Special Concerns – Inhalant use is a dangerous form of drug abuse. Many of the chemicals that are abused as inhalants are combined with other volatile and dangerous chemicals. Thus, when the inhalant abuser uses the substance, they experience serious physical and psychological injuries through exposure to other chemicals. For example Freon, a commonly used inhalant, is a refrigerant that produces extremely cold temperatures and is capable of freezing an adolescent's lungs so that they cannot breath.

Products That Are Frequently Abused As Inhalants . . .

Adhesives such as false-eyelash adhesives and fingernail adhesives, adhesives used in buildings, i.e., plastic and wood adhesive and plasic pipe adhesives.

Automotive engine cleaning agents and cleaners such as engine cleaners, auto-body cleaners, electronic and equipment cleaners, window cleaners, and gun cleaning solvents.

Beauty Products such as fingernail polish, fingernail polish remover, fingernail cement, fingernail hardener, aerosol hairspray.

Cements and Glues such as rubber cement, model glue, household cements, and shoe-sole glues.

Coating Agents such as frypan/cooking coatings, and aerosol leather/vinyl coatings.

Fluids such as typing-correction fluids, copier fluids, lighter fluids, brake/power steering/transmission fluids, Freon (air conditioning fluid), fire extinguisher fluids.

Gasoline such as car gas, gasoline additives and gas line antifreeze, camping lantern and stove fuels.

Paints and Paint Removers such as spray paint, clear acrylic paints, lacquer/varnish, paint removers and strippers, enamel paint, including furniture/wood stains and refinishers.

Magic Markers and Pens such as dry erase markers and felt tip pens, or any brand of fast drying markers.

Solvents such as tar removers, asphalt removers, paint thinner, household cleaning supplies with a solvent base.

Steroids

Steroids are a class of drugs which produce changes in the thinking, mood, and attitude of the user, as well as physical changes. Steroids are synthetic drugs that mimic hormones such as testsoterone. Changes in mood and personality are not a primary effect of the drug, but an undesireable side effect. This classification of drugs is included here because of the rising number of abuse cases on the part of student athletes.

Steroids

Drug Name	Street Name	What Does It Look Like?	Method of Use	What To Look For	Dangers and Harmful Effects
Anabolic Steroids: Clostebol Methandienone Fluoxy Mesterone Mesterolone Northandrolone Methenolone Nandrolone Oxymetholone Oxandrolone Oxymesterone Stanozolol Testosterone	Roids Juice Go Juice	Tablets Capsules Liquid for Injection	Taken in oral form or injected by hypodermic needle	Mood swings Temper outbursts Depression Aggressive or Violent behavior Increase in muscle mass over short period of time	There are over 70 side effects associated with steroid use including: Unpredictable effects on mood, thinking, and personality. Heart disease, liver damage, kidney damage, rashes, sexual disorders, delusions, paranoia, and combative-assaultive behavior.

Anabolic-Androgenic Steroids

***Historical Perspective* –** Anabolic-androgenic steroids are used in medicine to delay male sexual development, treat anemia, and certain types of cancer. Anabolic-androgenic steroid use among high school students is on the rise as student athletes begin to compete fiercely for sporting scholarships and recognition as they enter the highly competitive college environment. Recently, the use of Anabolic-androgenic steroids in preparation for athletic competition has come into focus as sporting committees have expelled athletes and stripped Olympic gold medals from well known athletes who have tested positive for steroid use.

The use of steroids in sporting competitions first became popular in the 1950's. Athletes used steroids believing that the drug increased body mass and strength, two important elements in sporting competition. There is conflicting evidence that steroids actually increase strength. Indeed, studies show that steroids improve the strength and performance in some athletes and not others. Although there are strict laws regulating the sale and use of steroids, they can be bought from physicians, coaches, mail order catalogs, friends, illegal laboratories and on the black market.

***Origin* –** Anabolic-androgenic steroids are synthetic analogs similar to the male hormone testosterone produced in the adrenal glands and testes.

***Street Names* –** Roids, Juice, Go Juice

***Route of Administration* –** Steroids can be taken orally in tablet or capsule form or by injection.

***Effects* –** Steroids have the ability to build tissue and have masculinizing properties. Most of the weight gained from steroid use comes from retained fluids and not from muscle buildup. Once steroid use is discontinued, the body weight and muscle gains quickly disappear. Use of Anabolic-androgenic steroids cause the body to decrease the production of testosterone.

What To Look For – Student athletes who feel the pressure of competition may be at high risk for Anabolic-androgenic steroid use. Steroid users may exhibit personality changes and as a parent you may begin to feel that the adolescent you are living with is becoming a stranger. Mood swings may be accompanied by temper outbursts and aggressive or violent behavior.

Long Term Effects – The use of steroids by adolescents can lead to serious side effects in both short and long term use. There are over 70 side effects associated with steroid use, including unpredictable changes in thinking, mood, and personality. For young males, steroid use can lead to frequent urination, shrunken testicles, and swollen prostrate. Young women may experience oily skin, hairiness, male pattern baldness, and menstrual disorders. Side effects for both young men and women include: heart disease, kidney damage, liver disease, rashes, sexual problems, combative or assaultive behavior, delusions and paranoia, and an increased risk of death. Changes in liver function include cirrhosis, jaundice, liver failure, and tumors. Anabolic-androgenic steroid users also experience an increased risk of injuries to ligaments, tendons, and muscles. Steroids may also increase the time it takes for an injury to heal.

Effects of Overdose – In even normal doses, steroid users may experience an adverse reaction which consists of weakness and a loss of consciousness. Research into the effects of high doses of steroids suggests that the user may suffer from fluid and sodium retention which can seriously upset the natural fluid and electrolyte balance of the body. High doses of steroids may also affect liver functioning. Anytime a parent suspects that an adolescent has taken a large dose of steroids, a physician should be consulted.

Withdrawal Symptoms – Anabolic-androgenic steroid users can develop dependence and find it difficult to stop using. Withdrawal symptoms include mild to severe depression, insominia, symptoms of mania, decrease in appetite and energy level, headaches and nausea. Withdrawal symptoms can last for up to three weeks after use is discontinued.

Designer Drugs

Designer drugs are manufactured illegally with a chemical formula that modifies the molecular structure of an illegal drug to produce analogs which can be sold legally. These drugs will imitate the illegal version, but are often a hundred times stronger and can have dangerous or fatal side effects.

DESIGNER DRUGS

Designer Drugs

Drug Name	Street Name	What Does It Look Like?	Method of Use	What To Look For	Dangers and Harmful Effects
Analogs of Methamphetamine and Amphetamine	MDMA (Ecstasy, XTC, Adam, Essence) MDM, PMA, STP	White Powder Tablets Capsules	Snorted (inhaled nasally) Taken orally Injected	Loss of appetite Decreased need for sleep Behavior changes Anxiety, Paranoia Aggressive behavior	Tremors Shakes Impaired speech Paralysis Brain damage
Analogs of Phencyclidine (PCP)	PCP (angel dust) PCE TCP	White Powder	Taken orally Injected Smoked or Snorted (inhaled nasally)	Dreamlike state Confusion Anxiety Fear of dying Slurred speech Blurred vision Uncoordination Assaultive behavior	Memory loss Inability to concentrate Insomnia Chronic or recurrent psychosis Death from accidents Death from overdose
Analogs of Fentanyl (Narcotic) **- or -** **Meperidine**	Synthetic Heroin China White Synthetic Heroin PEPAP MPTP MPPP	White Powder White Powder	Taken orally Injected Snorted (inhaled nasally)	Slow shallow breathing Cold clammy skin Constricted pupils Apathy Poor concentration Intoxicated behavior	Memory impairment Loss of coordination Accidents and injuries Respiratory failure Brain damage Coma Death

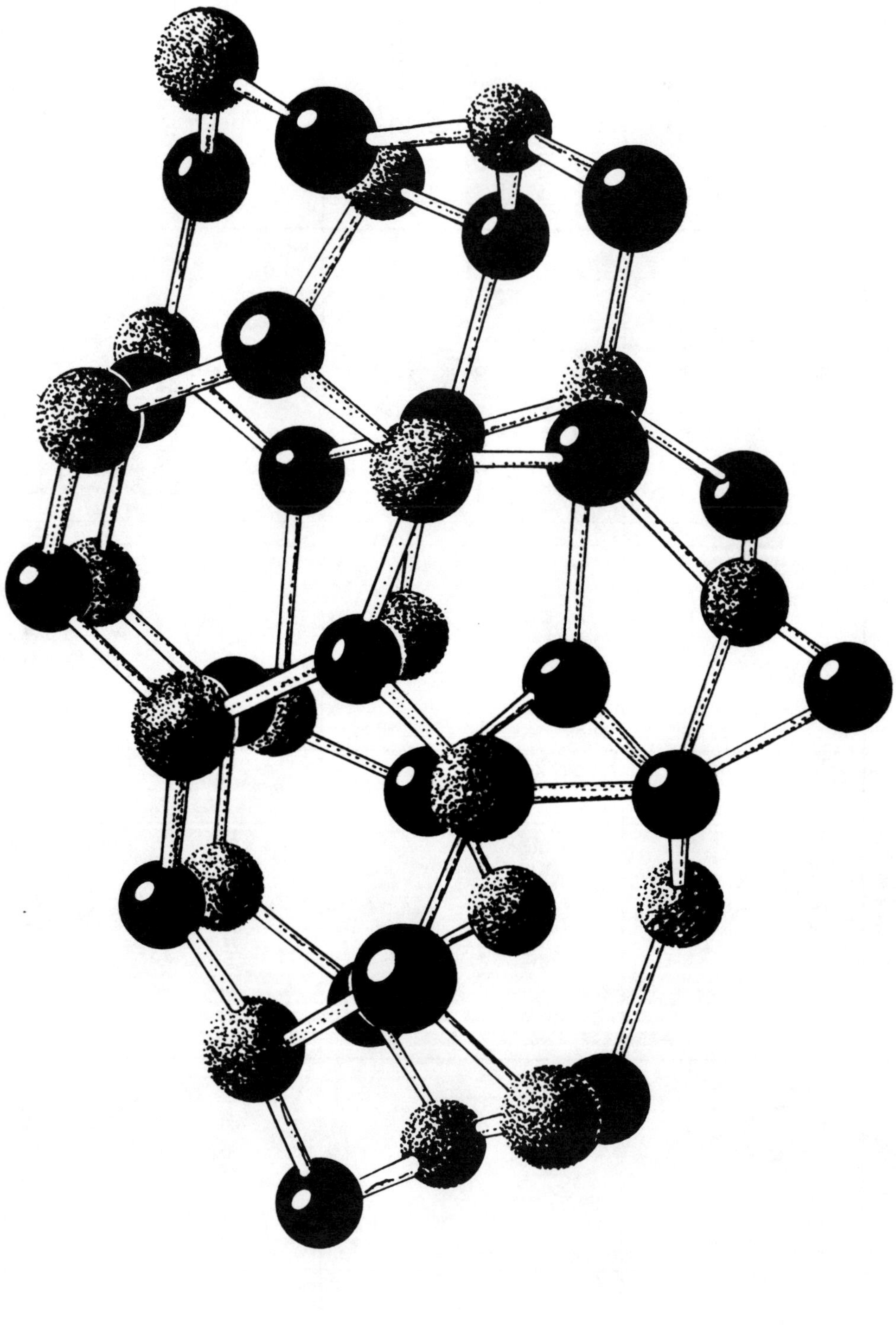

Designer Drugs

Origin **–** Designer drugs are analogs manufactured in underground laboratories from compounds that are not illegal. The designer drug mimics the actions of an illegal drug. Because the compound is not structurally identical to the drug compound it mimics, it is not illegal to manufacture or distribute. Each time government outlaws an analog, chemists take it back into the laboratory and change its molecular structure. Once the molecular structure is changed, the newly created analog can again be manufactured and distributed, a clear attempt to circumvent the law.

An example of an analog is the drug Ecstasy (3,4-Methylenedioxymethamphetamine (or) MDMA).

Street Names – Ecstasy, ETC, Adam, Essence

Route of Administration **–** Ecstasy (MDMA) may be snorted (inhaled nasally), taken orally, or by injection. The drug comes in powder, capsule and tablet form.

Effects **–** MDMA is described as a cross between the hallucinogen mescaline and the stimulant amphetamine. MDMA lowers anxiety levels in most people and causes them to feel less defensive. According to some psychotherapists who advocate the use of the drug in therapy, the drug lowers defensiveness, promotes empathy, and improves communication skills. The initial effects of the drug occur within 15 minutes, when the user experiences 15 minutes of sweating, eye oscillation, and an increase in heart rate and blood pressure. The user then experiences about 4 hours of contentment, insight, and self-acceptance, without the cognitive distortions of other drugs. After coming down, the user experiences about 24 hours of fatigue and a decreased appetite.

What To Look For **–** Because analogs mimic the effects of specific drugs including hallucinogens, amphetamines, narcotics, and PCP, it is important to know the signs and symptoms of these various drug categories.

Long Term Effects **–** The structure of analogs are unstable and unpredictable. Some of these drugs are reported to produce symptoms such as tremors and shakes, paralysis, drooling, impaired speech, and brain damage.

Effects of Overdose **–** According to the National Institute on Drug Abuse, analogs are reported to be responsible for over 100 deaths between 1983 and 1985, as well as hundreds of hospital emergency room visits. Effects of overdose range from anxiety and paranoia to paralysis and permanent brain damage. It should be noted that these effects can be caused by low doses and have occurred in first time users.

Unit Review - V.

✎ *Circle the correct answer . . .*

❶ The average age of an Inhalant abuser is . . .

A. 7 years old
B. $13^1/_2$ years old
C. $12^1/_2$ years old
D. 17 years old

❷ Inhalants may alter the perceptions of the abuser leading to delusions, hallucinations, and an altered perception of reality.

A. True
B. False

❸ According to the National Institute on Drug Abuse, analogs are reported to be responsible for over ________ deaths between 1983 and 1985.

A. 62
B. Over a hundred
C. 250
D. 18

❹ Ecstasy is described as a cross between the hallucinogen mescaline and the stimulant amphetamine. Esctasy is the drug . . .

A. PCP
B. MDMA
C. AMDA
D. LSD

❺ Athletes have used steroids in the belief that the drug increases . . .

A. Strength
B. Body mass
C. Their good looks
D. Strength and body mass

❻ Steroid use may ________ the time it takes for an injury to heal.

A. Decrease
B. Increase

❼ The high produced by most inhalants can last anywhere from . . .

A. 20 to 25 minutes
B. 1 to 2 hours
C. 2 to 4 hours
D. 1 minute to 1 hour

Answers found on Page 203

The Enemy Takes Over

The Assault

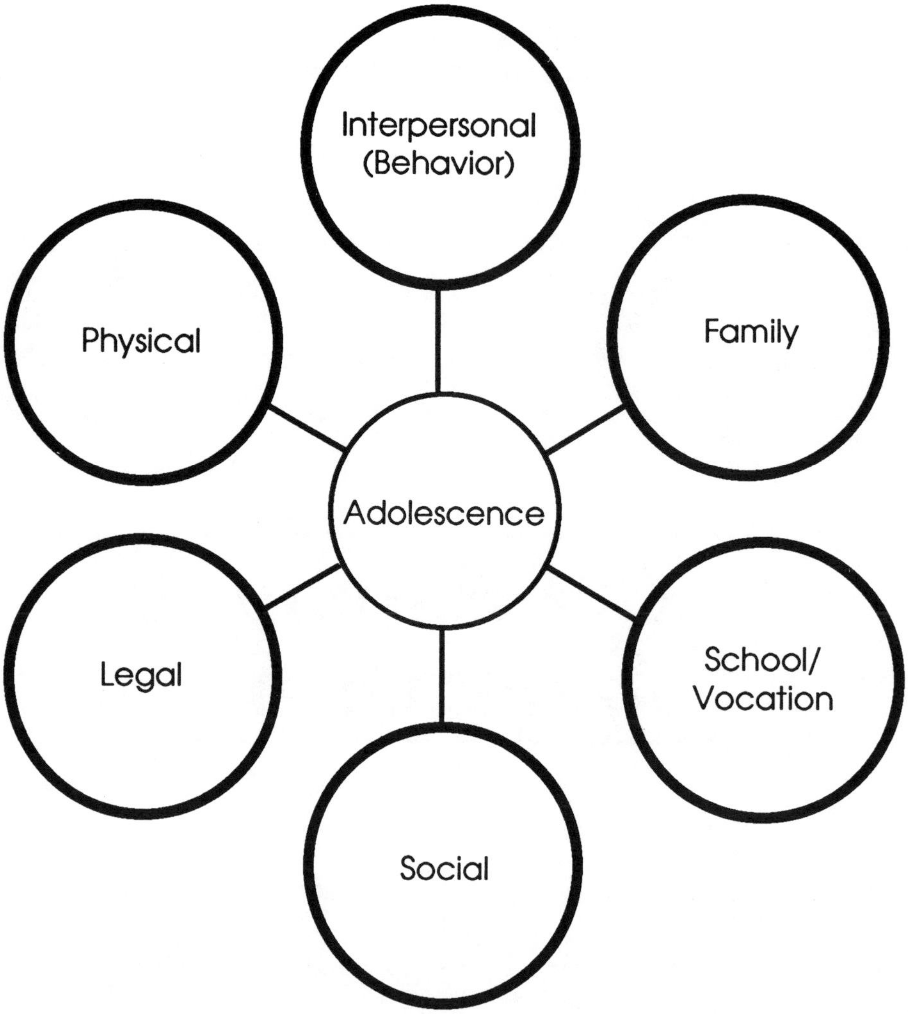

Six areas make up the world of the adolescent. Alcohol/drug use has a profound impact on each of these life areas. The more serious the abuse, the more serious the impact in each life area. Some areas may be impacted more seriously than other areas. For some adolescents, experiencing small consequences is enough to encourage them to change their behavior and cease alcohol/drug use while others can experience the most serious of consequences and yet not change their behavior.

Let us examine these areas separately:

I. Behavior Changes

As alcohol/drug use escalates in frequency and amount, the adolescent's behavior changes. Indicators of interpersonal impairment as a result of alcohol/drug use include . . .

***Using To Get Drunk/High/ Stoned* –** Abusing and drug dependent adolescents develop the attitude that the sole purpose for using alcohol/drugs is to achieve the high. Intoxication becomes the desired state of being.

***Using To Deal With Feelings* –** When using alcohol/drugs becomes a coping skill, two feelings that are often reported as the prime motivators for use are the need to belong and anger accompaning hurtful situations. Adolescents who feel inadequate around their peers quickly find that alcohol/ drugs remove feelings of fear or inhibition and help them deal with painful or traumatic events such as death, divorce, or other losses.

***Guilt Feelings For Use and Related Behaviors* –** Deception becomes a way of life for alcohol/drug using adolescents. If they are honest with their parents about their use, they risk consequences and restriction from friends and sources of alcohol/drugs. In the beginning, they think they are smarter than their parents and lie about their use. They find themselves involved in behaviors that they would not ordinarily. This creates internal conflict and leads to feelings of guilt and shame that fuel further use.

***Low Self Worth* –** This is a double edged sword for adolescents. Some adolescents have little or no self worth and get involved in alcohol/drug use to prop up their self esteem. Other adolescents experience a deterioration in self worth as they become involved in alcohol/drug use, especially if using is a major violation of their value system. For both groups of adolescents the result is the same: alcohol/drug abuse destroys self worth and clouds an adolescent's identity.

***Moral Deterioration/Values Change* –** Often easy for parents to identify, the adolescent becomes involved in behaviors that they would not ordinarily be involved with. They may steal from family, friends, or stores. They may become involved in promiscuity or sexual acting out. They begin to seriously violate family rules and there is a change in classroom behavior. The adolescent's well being begins to be at risk.

***Preoccupation With Using* –** As the adolescent moves deeper into abuse and closer to dependency, the drug becomes more and more important. Their lifestyle starts to reflect this shift in thinking. The beer bottle collection, the drug related clothing, earrings, the music that reflects a drug theme all are indicators of preoccupation. They report that they think about using in school, when they are with their parents, in church, and at other times when their minds should be on something else.

***Protecting Supply* –** It is natural for adolescents to hide their drug supply from their parents; yet it is not natural for them to hide their supply from each other. Soon they want to use up the supply of others before using their own, or deny having a supply in order to get it from others. They may sneak off at a party to use without sharing.

***Runaway Ideation or Attempts* –** As life becomes more hectic, fast paced, and seemingly out of control, running away becomes more and more of an option. In the beginning, the alcohol/ drug provided emotional escape but in the end it creates problems to escape from. Runaway behavior can become a device for manipulating parents. It is a scary situation for parents when an adolescent threatens, "Hassle me or ground me and I'll run away."

***Mood Swings* –** The adolescent who is involved in an abuse cycle begins to experience serious mood fluctuations. The adolescent who was once witty and outgoing suddenly becomes sullen and irritable. The slightest incident can send them into a tirade that can include profanity and physical aggression.

***Suicidal Ideation or Attempts* –** This behavior becomes, like running away, a coping method. Whether a true desire to end it all, or just a manipulation of parents, this is the most frightening situation parents face when dealing with their adolescent. It is not uncommon for parents to experience feelings of helplessness when dealing with suicidal behavior.

II. Family Problems

Family relationships are dramatically affected by an adolescent's alcohol/drug use. Indicators of family impairment include . . .

Breakdown in Communications – Communication for using adolescents can become a series of lies and cover ups. Secret keeping drives a wedge between family members especially if other siblings are aware of the alcohol/drug useage and they help cover it up. Parents begin to lose trust when messages are contradictory and confusing. As lies are uncovered, family stress and conflict increases.

Increased Negative Relations with Family Members – Broken family rules, theft and lies begin to stress and distort relationships as the abuser begins to lose control. Roles within the family shift to accommodate the confusing and inconsistent behavior of the using adolescent. Tension mounts and arguments increase, not only between adolescent and parent, but parent and parent. Often the source of the stress is not accurately identified as the alcohol/drug use; and families get into a cycle of blame as they try to understand these changes.

Threatened or Actual Loss of Family – This is the ultimate end result of out of control using and behavior on the part of the adolescent. Families reach a point where they believe they have run out of resources (emotional and financial) and turn their children over to foster care, state youth authorities and social service agencies. In some cases, the legal involvement of the adolescent is so extensive that the state assumes custody and incarcerates the adolescent.

III. Social Problems

Social relationships are affected by an adolescent's alcohol/drug use. Indicators of social impairment include . . .

Surrounds Self with Others Who Use the Same Way **–** Friends are a good indicator of where your child is at. Peer relationships are very important to the adolescent. As they move into experimental and abusive drug usage they tend to change friends and move into a friendship pattern that centers around alcohol/drug use. Peer pressure is one of the major factors that lead adolescents to first experimenting with alcohol/drugs. Although as a parent you can't pick your child's friends for them, you can monitor who they are out with. If you start hearing about individuals who are experiencing problems with the juvenile courts or have been in drug treatment programs themselves, this is a good indicator that your child is heading down the wrong road.

Inability To Have Sober Fun **–** Marked by an adolescent's inability to participate in normal social activities, fun is now not fun without alcohol/drugs. The adolescent has moved to a point where the alcohol/drug useage and related behaviors are exciting to them. Non-using situations do not provide the same type of stimulation so they seek situations where alcohol/drug usage are part of having fun.

Loss of Interest or Motivation in Previous Activities **–** As alcohol/drug use increases and the abuse cycle moves toward dependency, the adolescent begins to lose interest in activities that they normally found fun and exciting. Some alcohol/drug substances produce amotivational behavior (i.e. marijuana). This is compounded by the attitude that rewards for being involved in specific activity are not great enough. The adolescent becomes apathetic.

Uses to Function in Social Situations **–** The adolescent begins to use alcohol/drug substances to function in social situations. We begin to see adolescents using alcohol/drug substances before going to parties, school dances, or football games. It makes them more comfortable in their social environment.

Rejection of Concerned Others **–** We begin to see friends turning away from the adolescent as their alcohol/drug use increases, and their behavior becomes more out of control. Non-using adolescents and adolescents in the experimental stage begin to see the out of control adolescent as a threat to them. The threat may be that their behavior will expose them and their using to the parents or authorities. It may be that the using adolescent's behavior is obnoxious, illegal, or violates social mores and norms within the peer group. Friends that they have grown up with and gone through school with, suddenly turn away. The adolescent has a number of excuses as to why, often saying they dropped the friend, or that this friend wasn't good enough for some reason.

IV. School and Work Problems

As the adolescent increases their alcohol/drug use, goals for the future begin to fade away. School and vocational impairment resulting from alcohol/drug use include . . .

Decrease in Performance – The adolescent begins to show a decrease in performance as alcohol/ drug use escalates. Many drugs interfere with the ability to perform normal tasks. Also, poor attitudes and low motivation influence decreased performance. The adolescent starts coming late to school, skipping school, skipping particular classes in school, failing to turn in assignments, and grades start to spiral downward. The school may begin to call the parents and increased attention is placed on the adolescent.

Skipping, Truancy, and Tardy – These all influence decreased performance, but in themselves are a problem for the using adolescent. The amount of time spent in the classroom is mandated by the school and law, violation brings the school into conflict with the adolescent.

Teachers and Counselors Expressing Concern – One of the things heard most often about adolescents who are abusing is that they are not living up to their potential. The schools, the teachers, and counselors identify the student as a behavior problem, as an amotivational student, or as not following through with the normal expectations of a student their age. The schools start alerting the parents, and at that time, parents can conflict with the schools as they try to understand the adolescent's behavior. The adolescent tends to play the school and the home against each other stating "the teachers don't like me, and it is their fault that I have problems at school." Parents often want to take the side of their adolescent out of love, loyalty, and knowledge of past academic ability.

Loss of Sports or Other Extracurricular Activities – Adolescents who are harmfully involved with alcohol/drug usage start dropping favorite activities. Students are also kicked out of extracurricular activities as they violate school alcohol/drug use policies. Schools are beginning to tolerate alcohol/drug use less and less, and are starting to act and react more consistently. This creates conflict for the adolescent as their lifestyle becomes centered on alcohol/drug usage.

V. Legal Problems

Legal concerns as a result of alcohol/drug use includes . . .

Alcohol/Drug Related Arrests – These are arrests that are directly related to the possession and use of an alcohol/drug substance, including driving while under the influence, minor in consumption, minor in possession, and possession of drugs or drug paraphernalia. This is the blatant manifestation of the alcohol/drug problem as adolescents are caught in the act of using.

Other Legal Charges – A number of adolescents seen in treatment centers come in with legal charges such as burglary, vandalism, theft of property, shoplifting, etc. A number of these arrests are directly related to alcohol/drug usage. Adolescents steal so that they can continue to support their alcohol/drug using lifestyle. The money goes for direct purchase of drugs, or rock and roll tapes, or t-shirts, etc. that promote a using lifestyle.

Unruly, Runaway, Incorrigible, or Delinquent Charges – Are often direct results of out of control, alcohol/drug using behavior. Anytime an out of control adolescent is involved in the legal system, it is important to ask about their alcohol/drug use and start looking for other signs that the adolescent is abusing. If you look at the adolescent's behavior, you'll often see a pattern of symptoms that indicate alcohol/drug use.

VI. Physical Problems

Physical concerns as a result of an adolescent's alcohol/drug use include . . .

Medical Problems Related to Alcohol/Drug Use – There are a number of direct medical symptoms related to alcohol/drug use. Medical problems include ulcers of the throat and stomach, sinus conditions, memory impairment, weight gain or loss, heart and liver damage, and brain damage. We now know that every system of the body is affected by alcohol/drug use.

Increased Tolerance – This is a physical phenomenon that takes place within the adolescent as their body adapts to having more of the alcohol/drug substance on board. It takes more of an alcohol/drug substance to achieve the same point of intoxication as time progresses; thus, the adolescent begins to use alcohol/drugs more often and in larger amounts.

Emergency Room Visits and Accidents that are Alcohol/Drug Related – Overdoses of alcohol, or other drug substances, and pass outs are serious emergency situations. Overdoses, automobile accidents, motorcycle accidents, skateboarding accidents, and swimming accidents can be a direct result of excessive or abusive use of an alcohol/drug.

Withdrawal – True withdrawal symptomology is cause for medical concern. Withdrawal from substances such as alcohol can include shakes, tremors, hallucinations, convulsions, and, in some cases, death. This is an important consideration for parents when looking at the extent of alcohol/drug use on the part of their adolescent. If they are using a substance and they are physically addicted, there will be a withdrawal process that will need to be monitored carefully.

Loss of Control

Loss of control is a clear indicator that an adolescent is harmfully involved with alcohol/drug use, and needs to be evaluated by a professional. Indicators of loss of control include . . .

Binges – Binges are using periods which last 18-24 hours or longer.

Blackouts – Blackouts are periods of amnesia where the adolescent does not remember the events, or parts of time, while they are using an alcohol/drug substance. This is a serious situation in that many adolescents are involved in behaviors that they cannot remember and it is very difficult to confront an adolescent about something they don't remember.

Rapid Ingestion – Rapid ingestion is a phenomenon that occurs with adolescents, as well as adults. They play drinking games or ingest alcohol/drugs in a very quick manner to achieve rapid intoxication. This is not social using.

Using Alone – As the abuse cycle progresses toward dependency, we find the adolescent using alcohol/drugs alone, drinking in their room, smoking pot in the bathroom or the backyard, or taking the car out for a drive around the block and coming back stoned. It is not normal for an individual to use alone.

Morning Use, Before School, During Lunch – Many adolescents caught in the abuse cycle are using alcohol/drugs at odd times during the day. They are using in the morning before school which deteriorates school performance. They are cutting school during lunch to go use and coming back stoned or not at all. Morning usage is a clear sign of loss of control.

Unplanned Use – Adolescents often attend social events where alcohol/drugs are present. Adolescents who cannot control their intake at these events, and did not go to those events planning to use, are demonstrating loss of control.

Failed Attempts to Limit or Control Intake, or Failed Attempts to Go on the Wagon – An adolescent who cannot limit their intake, or cannot abstain from alcohol/drug usage after making promises to do so, has lost control over alcohol/drug usage.

Violence, or Threats of Violence, While Intoxicated – Adolescents who experience violence while intoxicated are a threat to themselves and to others. They can destroy property and can hurt themselves or others. It's important that this be taken very seriously, because violent alcohol/drug use behavior is an end stage of out of control usage.

Accidents – Accidents account for a number of hospitalizations on the part of adolescents. Adolescents who are abusing alcohol/drugs are accident prone, including automobile accidents, snowmobile accidents, broken legs (or other limbs), and falls down stairs. A number of life threatening drug related accidents are written off as just that, accidents. When parents explore their behavior further, they find out that there was alcohol/drug use involved. Anytime your adolescent is experiencing a series of accidents it is important to look at all the evidence and determine if there is a pattern.

Sign of the Times?

✎ Below are warning signs that indicate alcohol/drug use. Place an ✘ in the box beside each warning sign that applies to your adolescent. Add up the ✘s in each section and place the total in the appropriate place.

Behavior Changes					
	Withdrawn behavior		Angry outbursts		Obscene language or gestures
	Depression		Strange behavior		Attention getting behavior
	Mood swings		Disorientation		Defensiveness
	Increased irritability		Difficulty remembering events		Talk of suicide
	Hyperactivity		Inappropriate giggling/laughter		Suicide attempt
	Hypersensitivity		Inappropriate response		
	Apathy		Fights with peers or siblings		
					Total

School or Work Problems					
	Decreased ability to solve problems		Inconsistent work		Skipping classes
	Shortened attention span		Cheating		Truancy
	Frequent sick calls		Inconsistent grades		Suspension or expulsion
	Deterioration of rapport		Drop in grades		Dropping out of school
	Blaming problem on teachers or boss		Decreased work or job performance		Fired from a job
	Change in classroom behavior		Tardiness		
					Total

Physical Problems					
	Sleeping in excessive amounts		Excessive runny nose or sniffling		Staggering or stumbling
	Unusual weight gain or loss		Frequent urination		Loss of coordination
	Nervousness		Sores around the nostrils		Hand tremors or shakiness
	Rapid speech		Excessive coughing		Physical injuries
	Puffiness around eyes		Vomiting flushed complexion		
	Bloodshot eyes		Slurred speech		
					Total

Parents may view adolescent behavior as "just a phase" that they will grow out of. When viewed as a group, inappropriate behavior may indicate a serious problem.

	Family Problems				
	Deterioration in family relationships		Increased conflict over minor issues		Violence or threats of violence
	Breakdown in communications		Withdraws from family life		Running away from home
	Consistent lying		Missing money or objects		
	Broken rules, curfews, etc.		Broken promises		
					Total

	Social Problems				
	Changing friends		Friends who are in legal trouble		Loss of interest in hobbies or extracurricular activities
	Loss of Friendships		Failing to get along in social situations		
	Friends who are users		Loss of rapport with family friends		
					Total

	Legal Problems				
	Truancy charges		Involvement in thefts		Driving while under the influence
	Possession of alcohol or drugs		Vandalism		Accidents while intoxicated
	Selling of alcohol or other drugs		Arrests for intoxication		
					Total

Write the totals for each section here:

Behavior Changes Total ________

School/Work Problems Total ________

Physical Problems Total ________

Family Problems Total ________

Social Problems Total ________

Legal Problems Total ________

The more warning signs you have checked off, the greater the chances your adolescent is harmfully involved with alcohol/drugs, or has other serious emotional problems.

Let's Get Serious For a Minute!

In addition to alcohol and drug abuse, adolescents can suffer from a number of significant problems that affect their emotional and physical development. It is important for parents and professionals alike to develop an awareness of these issues. If an adolescent you know is experiencing any of these problems, seek professional help. Some of these disorders are life threatening.

Attention Deficit Disorder is characterized by impulsive behavior or a short attention span. In spite of best intentions, they are not capable of following through with appropriate behavior over long periods of time. They are easily distracted, have difficulty following a series of instructions (or their parents and teachers requests), have difficulty with school work and the organization of information, and act without thinking. Adolescents with ADD are also hyperactive, displaying fidgety and restless behavior. ADD can have negative effects on the adolescent as they attempt to function at home, school, and with their peer group. Attention deficit disorders are 10 times more common in boys than in girls.

Hyperactivity is characterized by excessive motor activity. The adolescent may have difficulty sitting quiet for even a short period of time, and is often restless, fidgety, and may talk excessively. Even during the sleep cycle, hyperactive children may move excessively. They have difficulty in school as they are disruptive to the teacher and other students. They may be labeled a troublemaker and are often the focus of discipline which can have an impact on their self concept and self esteem.

Learning Disabilities are often difficult to detect in children and adolescents. Each person is different in their development and learning processes. Learning disabilities vary widely from adolescent to adolescent and each disability is unique. Signs of a learning disability include an adolescent's inability to follow a set of simple instructions, difficulty grasping age appropriate concepts, lack of coordination, difficulty with switching letters or symbols, and an intense frustration with school. Adolescents who are experiencing learning disabilities need help and support at school and home. Gone undetected or untreated, learning disabled adolescents develop intense frustration with school and are at very high risk for acting out or drop out behavior.

Anorexia Nervosa is an eating disorder steming from an individual's refusal to eat, which leads to weight loss of at least 25 percent of body weight. Found primarily in young women, the disorder is linked to irrational beliefs that they are fat regardless of how thin they become. Their fear of becoming fat does not change with their change in body weight. Adolescents suffering from this disorder have a low self concept and poor self esteem. This disorder is difficult to treat and without treatment, some of these adolescents will die.

Bulimia is also an eating disorder which is found primarily in women. An adolescent may experience difficulties with both anorexia and bulimia and may struggle long into adulthood with these disorders. Bulimia is a compulsive behavior where the adolescent binges on a large amount of food (usually high calorie junk food) in a short period of time, and then rids the body of the food by self induced vomiting or laxatives. Weight fluctuations of 10 pounds or more may accompany this behavior. Binge/purge behaviors have serious implications for the adolescent and can have long term effects on their general health and development.

Depression is a mental illness that affects millions of Americans yearly. It is a disorder that produces a disturbance of mood and can produce a slowing of motor activity. Adolescents who are depressed may experience feelings of sadness, worthlessness, hopelessness, inappropriate guilt, irritability, a change in appetite with either a significant weight loss or gain, loss of energy, inability to think or concentrate, a significant disturbance of sleep, including inability to sleep or excessive sleeping, and recurring thoughts of suicide or death.

Manic Depression is a depressive disorder in which the individual fluctuates between periods of depression and periods of extreme euphoria or elation. When the adolescent experiences the depressive cycle of this illness, they exhibit the same symptoms as those listed under depression. When they are in the manic phase of this illness, they are easily excited, have an inappropriate elevation of mood, increased psychomotor activity, and may become hyperactive. When manic, the adolescent experiences excessively high self-esteem and may become involved in grandiose behavior or thinking.

Schizophrenia is a group of mental disorders characterized by problems in thought, feelings, and behavior accompanied with psychosis. In order for an adolescent to be diagnosed as having this disorder the symptoms must persist for more than six months. Symptoms include hallucinations, inappropriate emotions, delusions and/or paranoia, feelings that people are out to get them. Onset of this illness usually occurs between the ages of 16 and 25.

Sexual Abuse of children and adolescents has a dramatic and profound impact on the mental health. Victims of sexual abuse usually develop a low self concept and may act out their feelings and emotions in an inappropriate or antisocial manner. They may develop sleep problems or nightmares, depression, become suicidal, become involved in self mutiliation, become withdrawn and secretive, act out agressively, or become seductive and promiscuous. It is estimated that one in four girls and one in six boys are sexually abused by age 18.

Suicide is the third leading cause of death in adolescents. Suicidal symptoms may include those listed under depression. Warning signs include verbal clues such as "I'm better off dead," "Nobody will even miss me," or giving away favorite possessions. Adolescents who have had close friends or acquaintances who have committed suicide are at high risk, also, adolescents who are suddenly feeling very cheerful after an extended period of feeling sad or depressed.

Conduct Disorder is the term used to describe a repetitive pattern of acting out or illegal behavior. This acting out behavior is much more serious than that of the average adolescent and may include thefts, vandalism, alcohol or drug abuse, promiscuity or sexually aggressive behavior, difficulty at home, and suspension or expulsion from school. This adolescent usually experiences low self esteem in spite of a "tough guy" image.

Make The Match

Match the following descriptive statements with the appropriate mental health concern by place the letter beside each statement.

_____ 1. Is characterized by a disturbance of mood and a slowing of motor activity, along with feelings of sadness, guilt, worthlessness, and hopelessness.

_____ 2. Is a term to describe acting out or illegal behavior of an adolescent that is more serious in nature than the average adolescent.

_____ 3. Is characterized by problems in thought, feelings, and emotions, and includes symptoms of delusions, hallucinations, inappropriate emotions, paranoia.

_____ 4. Is characterized by an adolescent's excessive motor activity, disruptive behavior, and restlessness.

_____ 5. Is the third leading cause of death in adolescence. Warning signs may include verbal cues.

_____ 6. Is characterized by binges of large amounts of food in a short period of time, followed by self induced vomiting or the use of laxatives.

_____ 7. Adolescents who experience this may develop sleep problems, depression, may become suicidal, withdrawn, or secretive, or become seductive and/or promiscuous.

_____ 8. Is characterized by an adolescent's mood fluctuations between depression and extreme euphoria or elation.

_____ 9. Is characterized by an adolescent's refusal to eat, and is linked to an irrational belief that they are fat no matter how thin they become.

_____10. Is characterized by an adolescent's impulsive behavior and short attention span.

_____11. Is characterized by an adolescent's inability to follow a set of simple instructions, frustration, lack of coordination, and poor school work.

A. Bulimia

B. Hyperactivity

C. Depression

D. Anorexia Nervosa

E. Manic Depression

F. Sexual Abuse

G. Schizophrenia

H. Conduct Disorder

I. Learning Disability

J. Attention Deficit Disorder

K. Suicide

Answers found on Page 203

Kids and Cons

Adolescents who are abusing alcohol or other drugs get good at making up stories to cover up their behavior and useage. Parents need not be suspicious about everything their adolescent is saying, but they will need to develop an awareness for repeated excuses and stories that don't follow logic.

The following is a sample of cons used by kids to cover up their behavior and alcohol/drug use.

Possession of alcohol/drugs . . .
- I'm holding it for a friend
- I don't know how it got there
- It's the first time I tried it
- I was just experimenting
- That isn't a pipe . . . It's an incense burner
- I didn't know it was drugs

Red eyes . . .
- I have dirt in my eyes
- I've been swimming
- I got soap in my eyes
- I've been crying (it was a sad movie)
- My contacts are bothering me
- I'm tired
- Wearing sunglasses (the light hurts my eyes)

Funny smells . . .
- My friends were smoking
- It is cigarette smoke
- I was burning incense
- I spilled cleaning fluid
- Someone poured beer on me
- Using breath mints or gum

Strange behavior . . .
- I'm sick (sleeping all the time)
- Watching T.V. in the dark
- Reading excessively
- Leaning on walls when walking or standing
- Munchies (snacking all the time)

Talkin' the talk . . .
- You're always accusing me!
- You're out to get me!
- Who me? I don't have a problem.
- They made me do it!
- I am sick (to get out of discussion)
- What's wrong . . . nothing!
- I never said that . . . you're crazy!
- That's not how it happened! (you're crazy)

Going places . . .
- I'm spending the night at a friend's
- I'm doing the football game (or other sport)
- Frequent or last minute plan changes
- I'm going to play video games
- I was just hanging out at the mall
- Went to a show

Denial ~ The Dangerous Defense

Denial is an emotional defense mechanism that can isolate parents from the pain of raising a difficult adolescent. Denial can be a necessary delaying device for parents as they struggle to cope with the reality of their adolescent's behavior and chemical use. Unfortunately, a parent's denial can stand between their adolescent and the help they need.

Examples of denial by parents:

It's just a phase.
My kid is too young to have a drug problem.
It's those rotten friends. They are bad influences.
Those other kids have a problem, not my child.
My kid is failing in school because the work is too hard (or too easy).
My kid is doing so well in school.
The police are out to get my adolescent.
It's not that big of a problem.
Change the subject.
Avoid the problem.

✍ What are the ways that you deny that your adolescent may be having problems?

____

____

____

____

____

____

____

As denial fades, it is replaced with anger. This anger can be expressed as accusations made toward the very people that are trying to help. Counselors, probation officers and court workers can often be the target of this anger as they may be the bearer of bad news.

Adolescents, as well as parents (or other family members), deny the reality of a situation even in the face of overwhelming facts to the contrary.

Examples of denial by adolescents:

I can quit anytime.

It's not that bad.

I'm too young to have a problem.

The school (teacher, coach, or police) lied to you.

How can I have a problem? I'm doing well in school.

Those aren't my drugs, I'm holding them for a friend.

I only had two beers (even if they are so drunk they can't stand).

Change the subject.

✍ What are some of the ways that your adolescent may deny that they are having problems?

___

___

___

___

___

___

___

___

___

Enabling: Operation Cover-Up

Enabling is one of the most common behaviors that parents become involved in. Simply put, enabling provides adolescents the opportunity to continue inappropriate behavior.

Parents are not responsible for the actions of their adolescents, but can unwittingly help adolescents continue their inappropriate behavior by covering it up, denying the problem, or taking away the opportunity to experience consequences. Parents need to look closely at what they get from enabling their adolescent, as well as what they may lose by enabling.

Examples of enabling behaviors:

Avoid confronting inappropriate behavior
Avoid sensitive issues by "walking on eggshells"
Ignore chemical use
Blame problems on adolescent's friends
Compare one child to another
Make excuses for their behavior to family, friends, school, law
Undermine spouse's attempts at discipline
Undermine attempts by others to help the adolescent
Drive around trying to find adolescent
Argue with spouse when angry with your adolescent
Let problems build instead of taking care of them when they occur
Cut back on social outings to stay home to "keep an eye on" the adolescent or protect the house

Take on adolescent's consequences
- Pay legal fines, speeding tickets, restitution
- Write notes to excuse tardiness or absences from school
- Call their boss to make excuses for them

Take on guilt for the problem
- If I were a good parent . . .
- If I were more strict . . .
- If I like their friends . . .

✍ Describe ways that you enable your adolescent.

✍ Describe what you stand to gain if you continue to enable your adolescent.

✍ Describe what you stand to lose if you continue to enable your adolescent.

In The Trenches

So . . . You think you're crazy!

Has your adolescent ever said to you . . . ?

"I never said that!

That isn't how it happened.

You must be crazy!"

Living with an out of control adolescent can leave you feeling crazy. They want to invalidate your feelings and convince you that what they're saying, doing, and feeling is accurate and that you are crazy. Parents can take this on and begin feeling out of control and indeed crazy. At times when parents need to be seeking professional advice for their adolescent, they instead seek professional advice for themselves as a result of feeling crazy.

Behavior Log

The purpose of the behavior log is to provide a factual listing of your child's behaviors that cause you concern. This is a reality check and will give you an opportunity to objectively look at your adolescent's behavior, your response to that behavior, and how you are left feeling about the behavior. This reality check helps you restore a feeling of control.

It's important to know that ***feeling*** out of control is not the same thing as ***being*** out of control. Often times, as we deal with the out of control feelings we have, we start getting back on track as effective parents. We start taking back our personal power, start asserting authority, and begin to draw boundaries and provide limits which are necessary for out of control adolescents.

If a series of behaviors or incidents are detailed in the behavior log, then a problem can be less easily denied (especially when the behaviors or incidents are tied to chemical use – the adolescent has a harder time denying a chemical problem). The behavior log contains four sections.

Section One: Date of the Behavior or Incident

It is important to be as accurate as possible in providing the date or season that the behavioral incident occurred. The goal here is to establish chronology and tie the behaviors to a time line, thus demonstrating that these behaviors are not (or are) random occurrences.

1

Date of the Incident or Behavior Day, Month, Year, or Season, or Grade			
Halloween of your ninth grade year			

If possible, give dates or seasons that they were involved in these incidents. It's often easiest to remember them in terms of developmental milestones or academic experiences. Using the seasons – fall, winter, spring and summer – is helpful. Using grades – 9th grade, 10th grade, 11th grade, etc. – is also helpful, especially if the behavior log extends over a period of several years.

When preparing the behavior log avoid using words like "always" or "sometimes" when dealing with these experiences. We know that no one "always" does something, and that "sometimes" circumstances are different. By using these two words, you do not get an accurate picture of the frequency or duration of the behaviors or incidents in question.

Section Two: The Behavior or Incident which caused you concern

It is important to describe the behavior or incident in factual terms. Avoid making interpretations about the adolescent's thinking, frame of mind or feelings during the particular behavioral incident.

2

Date of the Incident or Behavior Day, Month, Year, or Season, or Grade	Incident or the behavior that caused you to be concerned **Be specific!**		
Halloween of your ninth grade year	You went to a party at a friend's house and got drunk and became sick on their new furniture		

Interpretations give the adolescent a point of argument. It is difficult for adolescents to argue with factual descriptions of behavior (i.e., they know they broke the lamp, or they know they threw the car keys across the house). It is easy for them to argue if you are making interpretations about what they think or feel. They are quick to use "point of view" to defocus from the behavior you want to address. This is especially important when you use this information in the context of an intervention.

Do not make excuses for the behavior or incident. By making excuses for the behavior, you discount the severity and impact that it has on you. It is not your fault that your adolescent chooses to behave this way, just as it is not your resonsibility to experience the consequences that accompany the behavior. These are two points that parents need to work through – ***denial*** of the problem and ***enabling*** the process to continue.

Section Three: Your actions in response to the Behavior or Incident

Your actions in response to the behavior or incident are important in providing a comprehensive picture of the situation and the actions and reactions that took place. It gives you an opportunity to look at your patterns of responding and how you are affected by the incident or the behavior in question.

3

Date of the Incident or Behavior Day, Month, Year, or Season, or Grade	Incident or the behavior that caused you to be concerned Be specific!	How you reacted to the Behavior/ Incident – Both verbal and non-verbal	
Halloween of your ninth grade year	You went to a party at a friend's house and got drunk and became sick on their new furniture	When I came to get you, I grabbed you and you fell down and got hurt. I yelled at you in front of your friends.	

If you find that there is a consistent pattern of responding on your part that is ineffective in dealing with your adolescent's behavior, or that in fact enables the adolescent's behavior, then it gives you an opportunity to make some constructive changes. Constructive changes in parenting strategies can often unbalance the situation and influence your adolescent to act differently, hopefully more appropriately.

Another important purpose of this section is to help you identify parenting strategies which are effective for you. When you are dealing with an adolescent who is escalating to a point of being out of control, you want to quickly identify those strategies which work and discontinue those strategies which do not. If your ineffective responses become predictable, the adolescent knows that they can manipulate you and the boundaries within the home. By the same token, if some of your responses are effective and are consistently used, this can draw boundaries for the adolescent and provide them with limits they need.

Section Four: Your feelings about the behavior or incident, and/or feelings about your response to the behavior or incident

Date of the Incident or Behavior Day, Month, Year, or Season, or Grade	Incident or the behavior that caused you to be concerned Be specific!	How you reacted to the Behavior/ Incident – Both verbal and non-verbal	4 How you felt about the Behavior/ Incident and how you felt about your reaction to it!
Halloween of your ninth grade year	You went to a party at a friend's house and got drunk and became sick on their new furniture	When I came to get you, I grabbed you and you fell down and got hurt. I yelled at you in front of your friends.	I was hurt and angry. I was embarrassed at the way I acted. I felt bad for you and your friends

This section is important to help you understand how you are feeling during the incident, or how you are left feeling after the incident is over. It also gives you a chance to see how your adolescent impacts you and can help you convey your feelings to the adolescent. Often, adolescents are unable to take the perspective of their parents on a feeling level. They don't understand the impact that their behavior has on others. Consult the feeling list at the end of this chapter for a list of common feelings and emotions.

If you feel that your adolescent is experiencing problems and you aren't sure if you are overreacting or not, keep a behavior log. Go back in your mind and write down past incidents that you can clearly remember.

If after a period of time you discover that your adolescent has a problem, enlist the assistance of a trained professional. Do not try to intervene yourself without professional help.

I was feeling . . .

Angry
Antagonistic
Hostile
Outraged
Furious
Irritated
Displeased
Revolted
Quarrelsome
Aggressive
Sarcastic
Rebellious
Defiant
Unaffectionate

Sad
Sorrowful
Depressed
Unhappy
Gloomy
Despairing
Grief stricken
Disinterested
Hopeless
Empty
Forlorn
Discouraged
Lonely

Afraid
Helpless
Terrified
Apprehensive
Anxious
Hesitant
Scared
Panicky
Worried
Pensive
Submissive
Watchful
Cautious

Happy
Cheerful
Hopeful
Ecstatic
Playful
Satisfied
Gleeful
Elated
Enthusiastic
Delighted
Affectionate
Sociable
Agreeable

Embarrassment
Ashamed
Humiliated
Embarrassed
Shy
Self conscious
Nervous
Meek
Guilty
Bashful
Timid
Rejected

Disgusted
Indignant
Intolerant
Annoyed
Loathful
Contemptuous
Unreceptive
Unfriendly
Critical
Bitter
Vengeful
Disatisfied
Unsympathetic
Uncooperative

Peaceful
Serene
Calm
Content
Pleased
Proud
Trusting
Tolerant
Interested
Generous
Attentive
Patient
Receptive

Confused
Perplexed
Bewildered
Indecisive
Vacillating
Puzzled
Ambivalent
Confused
Apathetic
Uncertain
Wondering

Curious
Daring
Inquisitive
Adventurous

Possessive
Jealous
Greedy
Suspicious
Distrustful
Demanding
Expectant
Resentful
Boastful

Behavior Log

Date of the Incident or Behavior Day, Month, Year, or Season or Grade	Incident or the Behavior that caused you to be concerned Be specific!	How you reacted to the Behavior/Incident Both verbal and non-verbal	How you felt about the Behavior/ Incident and how you felt about your reaction to it!

Behavior Log

Date of the Incident or Behavior Day, Month, Year, or Season or Grade	Incident or the Behavior that caused you to be concerned Be specific!	How you reacted to the Behavior/Incident Both verbal and non-verbal	How you felt about the Behavior/ Incident and how you felt about your reaction to it!

Behavior Log

Date of the Incident or Behavior Day, Month, Year, or Season or Grade	Incident or the Behavior that caused you to be concerned Be specific!	How you reacted to the Behavior/Incident Both verbal and non-verbal	How you felt about the Behavior/ Incident and how you felt about your reaction to it!

Behavior Log

Date of the Incident or Behavior Day, Month, Year, or Season or Grade	Incident or the Behavior that caused you to be concerned Be specific!	How you reacted to the Behavior/Incident Both verbal and non-verbal	How you felt about the Behavior/ Incident and how you felt about your reaction to it!

Behavior Log

Date of the Incident or Behavior Day, Month, Year, or Season or Grade	Incident or the Behavior that caused you to be concerned Be specific!	How you reacted to the Behavior/Incident Both verbal and non-verbal	How you felt about the Behavior/ Incident and how you felt about your reaction to it!

Behavior Log

Date of the Incident or Behavior Day, Month, Year, or Season or Grade	Incident or the Behavior that caused you to be concerned Be specific!	How you reacted to the Behavior/Incident Both verbal and non-verbal	How you felt about the Behavior/ Incident and how you felt about your reaction to it!

Behavior Log

Date of the Incident or Behavior Day, Month, Year, or Season or Grade	Incident or the Behavior that caused you to be concerned Be specific!	How you reacted to the Behavior/Incident Both verbal and non-verbal	How you felt about the Behavior/ Incident and how you felt about your reaction to it!

Is It Possible to Love an Adolescent?

At one time or another your adolescent is going to rub you the wrong way. Parenting a difficult adolescent can be painful. After all, when you are the parent, you have to deal with the adolescent everyday. You want him/her to grow up right, and you feel responsible for his/her actions as well as your own.

Pinpoint what you don't like about the adolescent's behavior and analyze why. Be as specific as you can. It is important to separate the behavior from the adolescent. Adolescents look for critical messages from adults and use them to define their self concept. If they sense that you do not like them as a person, they will rebel against authority out of hurt and anger.

Focus on the behavior that you don't like and not on the adolescent. The job of the parent is to give unconditional love and acceptance in spite of the adolescent's personal habits, dress, music, or friends.

✍ List your adolescent's behaviors that rub you the wrong way.

____

____

____

____

____

Make a special effort to be fair. Treat the adolescent fairly and consistently. Let them know what you like about their behavior, as much as what you don't. Don't hold their behavior against them for long periods of time. Don't drag out punishments or consequences.

✍ Describe a time you dealt unfairly with your adolescent.

____

____

____

____

____

Make a list of the adolescent's good qualities. Spend time with the adolescent and get to know their good qualities. Help the adolescent identify their assets and strengths. Let them know that you notice these strengths. Praise them in public. This encourages them to do better.

✍ What are some of your adolescent's good qualities?

____

____

____

____

____

Get more involved with your adolescent. We all have a tendency to avoid our adolescent if encounters with them are stressful or full of conflict. This can reinforce their feelings of low self worth. Make a conscious effort to spend time with your adolescent. Talk to them, get involved in their life (but don't try to run it), and most of all listen to them. They will respond positively if they feel listened to.

✍ How can you spend time with your adolescent to promote a better relationship with them?

____

____

____

____

____

Look to the future. Don't look back into the past and keep reminding your adolescent of the things they did. Once you have addressed the behavior that you don't like, step back and give them a chance to change it. Remember not to hold their past behavior against them. They need to make mistakes, learn from them and change. They need your unconditional love, acceptance and encouragement.

These are not magic solutions to the problems that you will face with your adolescent. However, if you do the things mentioned here, and do them honestly, your acceptance of your adolescent will grow, and your anger will fade. Your adolescent will be a lot easier to parent and you will be easier for the adolescent to accept and like.

How Well Do You Listen to Your Adolescent?

When life is pressing you and the bills need to get paid and the boss is hasseling you for more overtime, it's hard to come home to the needs and demands of an adolescent. When times are tough, it is hard to be a good listener. Unfortunately, that's just the time your adolescent is going to need you to be a good listener.

✎ Answer each question below by circling the answer that best describes your listening skills with your adolescent. When your adolescent approaches you to talk do you . . .

1. Prepare yourself physically by putting down the paper, turning off the t.v. or radio, or stopping the activity you are engaged in, so you can hear?

never *occasionally* *often* *always*

2. Watch your adolescent for nonverbal cues, as well as listen to what is said?

never *occasionally* *often* *always*

3. Decide from their appearance if they are saying something important?

never *occasionally* *often* *always*

4. Interrupt if you feel they have said something wrong?

never *occasionally* *often* *always*

5. Try to have the last word?

never *occasionally* *often* *always*

6. Ask clarifying question such as: "Is this what you are saying", or "What I heard you say is . . . "?

never *occasionally* *often* *always*

7. Listen for feelings, as well as thoughts and ideas?

never *occasionally* *often* *always*

8. Give thought to what is said before responding to requests?

never *occasionally* *often* *always*

9. Offer encouragement to your adolescent while they are talking to you?

never *occasionally* *often* *always*

10. Listen to what your adolescent is trying to say as well as what they are actually saying?

never *occasionally* *often* *always*

After answering the questions, how would you rate yourself as a listener with your adolescent?

Poor ***Fair*** ***Good*** ***Excellent***

Being a good listener takes a conscious effort on the part of parents. Parents need to tune into their adolescents and understand what the adolescent is trying to tell them about their experiences and problems. Listening to a troubled adolescent takes even more effort and energy, but is vitally important to their safety and well-being. Many times they are trying to tell us something but we may not be listening in a way that promotes understanding. Good communication is built on good listening. We need to be role models for our adolescents.

There is More to Saying "*No*" Than Just a Word

As a parent, you are required to put limits on your adolescent's behavior. Part of successfully setting limits is learning to say "no". Saying "no" can be uncomfortable, and parents may feel unpopular with their adolescent. It is important that parents learn to say "no" effectively so the adolescent can learn to grow up with rules and expectations.

Explain why you must say "no" to their behavior or request. By letting them know why you are saying "no", you can teach them how to think critically and objectively about issues. Using reasons such as "I'm the parent", or "Because I said so" promotes a power struggle. It is important to stay out of power struggles with an adolescent. Once you have explained your position, you do not have to repeat your explanation or defend your decision.

Let your adolescent know under what conditions a "no" might be reconsidered. By letting your adolescent know that a request has merit but certain conditions must be met before you can say yes, you give them incentive for change and improvement. It lets them know what your standards are and how they can meet them.

Say "no" consistently. Don't be wishy washy. Don't say yes when you mean to say "no". Maintain consistent standards and expectations. If you change the rules of behavior frequently, your adolescent may become confused and angry. Adolescents, especially troubled adolescents, need consistent guidelines when growing up.

✍ List several times when you said "yes", but really wanted to say "no".

____

____

____

____

____

____

____

Pick the right time and place to say "no". Avoid saying "no" when you are feeling under pressure or uptight. Tell your adolescent you want to take some time to think about your decision. Then set a time when you can both get together to discuss it again. Then follow through. Be careful if you feel you are being pushed into a confrontation, especially in front of your adolescent's friends. Parents seldom win a power struggle.

✍ How does your adolescent try to manipulate you into saying "yes" when you have said "no"?

____

____

____

____

____

Stand up for your right to say "no". You are the parent and have the right to say "no". Don't be manipulated into feeling guilty when looking out for the best interests of your adolescent. You are a competent human being capable of making good decisions. Your adolescent may try to guilt you into saying "yes".

✍ What are some things that you would like to do differently when saying "no" to your adolescent.

____

____

____

____

____

Be willing to say "no" to the behavior or request, not the adolescent. The idea may be bad, not the adolescent. Be fair and flexible. Re-evaluate your decision to say "no" as the adolescent proves that he/she can handle more responsibility. Don't hold the past against them but use it as a teaching tool to help them develop responsibility. Praise their resourcefulness and encourage them to keep trying.

Taking Charge

Draw the Line

Adolescents need to know clearly and concisely your position toward alcohol and other drug use. Parents need to take a position of "no use" with their adolescent. The risk to psychological, physical, spiritual and social development makes any use of alcohol/drugs by an adolescent inappropriate. If parents do not set clear guidelines and expectations, as well as consequences for violating the "no use" policy, parents send an unclear message to kids about how they should respond to alcohol/drug situations.

Use the following worksheet to formulate your policy statement concerning alcohol/drug use.

✍ What are the expectations and guidelines for the adolescent in our family to remain alcohol/drug free? (Expectations must be clearly defined in simple concise terms that everyone can understand.)

____

____

____

____

____

✍ How will this policy be monitored (without being a spy, a snoop, a sneak, or driving yourself nuts with paranoia)?

____

____

____

____

____

____

✍ What are the consequences and how will they be enforced?

☞ Positive consequences for following through with the policy (acknowledge compliance, support them in the struggle to resist peer pressure, and reward their efforts to remain alcohol/drug free).

____

____

____

____

____

☞ Negative consequences for not following the policy to remain alcohol/drug free (consequences that are appropriate to the situation, consistently held and enforced, and moderate).

____

____

____

____

____

✍ How will we communicate these guidelines and expectations to our adolescent? (So they can understand them and there will be no misunderstanding of exactly what is expected, or what the positive and negative consequences will be.)

____

____

____

____

____

The Plan

The goal of this section is to help you plan out responses to behaviors and incidents that can be expected from an adolescent (especially one who is acting out of control). The objective is to prevent incidents from becoming a crisis. If you are in crisis, chances are that you will make hasty decisions that you will regret later. When parents are in crisis they do not parent effectively. Decisions are made under pressure and not well thought out. Parenting becomes reactive and not pro-active. The adolescent can catch parents off balance and take control by manipulating situations, feelings and emotions.

By thinking through possible problems and making a plan to deal with these incidents, we can approach behaviors and incidents with relative calm. We can take charge of a situation and avoid being manipulated or blackmailed into a response.

DEALING WITH THE HIGH TIMES!

It is inevitable that at some point your adolescent will come home and you will know that they have been experimenting with alcohol/drugs. How you react to that situation can have a tremendous impact on the future attitude of your adolescent. Asking your adolescent to get up early the next day to clean the entire house is not an effective approach to deterring future alcohol use. Plan out your response so that you may use these situations to teach your adolescent about your values and attitudes toward alcohol/drug use.

Respond to the following situations as completely as you can.

✍ You find a six pack of beer in your child's closet. You would . . .

____

____

____

____

____

____

✍ Your child begins to hang around several kids who have been in trouble with the law and are suspected of using drugs. You would . . .

____

____

____

____

____

✍ You leave your 17 year old adolescent home alone for two days while you attend the funeral of a distant relative. Upon returning home, you notice that the garbage can is full of beer cans, a lamp is broken, and several pieces of jewelry are missing. You would . . .

____

____

____

____

____

✍ Your adolescent asks permission to go to a party at a friends's house that is to be chaperoned by an adult. You instruct your adolescent to be home at midnight. Your adolescent comes home at 1:30 a.m. and is intoxicated. You would . . .

____

____

____

____

____

THE SUICIDE SOLUTION?

A suicide threat or attempt is a serious issue for adolescents and their parents. Suicidal behavior or threats can provide the family with the perfect opportunity for crisis. Parents who feel that suicide may be an issue for their adolescent need to plan a response to this behavior. As a parent it may be difficult to determine if the threat is real or if it is manipulation. Any suicidal threat or gesture on the part of an adolescent needs to be taken seriously.

✍ If I think my adolescent is suicidal or if my adolescent makes a suicide threat, I will . . .

____

____

____

____

____

____

____

____

____

✍ Who are the mental health professionals I can call if I think my adolescent is suicidal or if my adolescent makes a suicide threat?

	Name	Telephone
1.		
2.		
3.		
4.		

ON THE RUN!

Running away places an adolescent at risk. Like a suicide attempt, it is a serious issue. Parents who feel that runaway behavior may be an issue need to plan a response to this behavior. As with a suicide threat, a parent may find it difficult to determine if a threat to run away is real or if it is manipulation.

✍ If my adolescent runs away I will . . .

____

____

____

____

____

✍ Who can I call if my adolescent is on the run?

	Name	Telephone
1.	____________________	____________
2.	____________________	____________

WALKING ON EGGSHELLS!

Living with an out of control adolescent can be a scary experience. At times, parents may fear for their personal safety as well as the safety of other family members in the home. We have the right to live in our homes free from fear of physical or emotional harm. A safety plan should include the safety of all family members, as well as their property.

✍ If my adolescent is threatening me or other family members, I will . . .

____

____

____

____

____

✍ If my adolescent damages any property in my home, I will . . .
(This includes punching holes in walls and doors, damaging furnishings, or stealing objects from the home).

____

____

____

____

____

STAYING IN TOUCH!

Support systems are important to the mental health of parents. As things heat up, our perceptions can become distorted, especially if our adolescent is trying to convince us that we are crazy. Parents with adolescents would do well to compare notes with other parents of adolescents. This can have a multitude of benefits including:

☞ Helping us to feel like there is someone out there who understands the struggles we are going through.

☞ Providing a reality check to affirm us as parents and reinforce our positive qualities.

☞ Comparing parenting strategies and techniques for dealing with a number of problems that seem to arise with adolescents.

✍ Who are the people who can provide you with support?

	Name	Telephone
1.	______________________	____________
2.	______________________	____________
3.	______________________	____________
4.	______________________	____________

✍ What type of activities can you participate in with other parents to gain support?

____

____

____

____

____

TAKE OUT A LITTLE INSURANCE!

It is possible to insure your house and property against the ravages of an adolescent's out of control behavior. If damage occurs, you can call your insurance company. It is difficult to provide the same insurance for your relationship with a spouse (lover or significant other).

As an adolescent begins to lose control, parents are often inclined to stay home, limit their social life, and 'guard the house'. Focus in the family shifts to the adolescent; they become the center of attention and activity. It is important to take care of your relationships and not allow the adolescent to become the center of the family. You can always buy new possessions but not new relationships.

✍ How do you allow your adolescent to affect your relationship with your spouse (lover or significant other)?

____

____

____

____

____

____

____

✍ How do you take care of your relationship with your spouse (lover or significant other)?

____

____

____

____

____

____

____

✍ As it relates to your adolescent, what would you like to do differently in your relationship with your spouse (lover or significant other)?

____

____

____

____

____

____

____

____

____

Personal Contract

Self Affirmation: *I am important and valuable to myself. I am a worthwhile human being. As a parent, I understand the importance of taking care of myself. If I do not take care of myself, I cannot take care of my family.*

✍ Below are listed the changes that I would like to make in my life. The changes I make will enhance my life, my happiness, and my well-being.

Personal	**Family**
Feelings/Emotions	**Spiritual**
Social/Recreational	**Hobbies**
Artistic Growth/Creativity	**Vocation/Education**

Make Them an Offer They Can't Refuse

Contracting is an effective means of intervention for out of control adolescents. This may seem absurd given the fact that your adolescent may be showing disregard for house rules, school responsibilities, may be lying, cheating, and stealing. To some parents, contracting with an adolescent may seem like a pact with the devil.

In order for contracting to be successful, parents have to understand some basic concepts about the contract and the contracting process.

What are you trying to change? It is important for you to begin the contracting process by considering the goals you want to accomplish. Do you want to control your adolescent or do you want your adolescent to modify their behavior in some particular way? If you are looking for control, the contract will not work. You will be more successful if you target certain behaviors that your adolescent can modify or change. Be specific with these behaviors. The more specific you are the better your adolescent can understand the expectations for change.

Offer a challenge. The contract works because the adolescent will agree to certain terms based on their erroneous belief that they can pull it together and hold it together. ***(A)*** The parent presents the notion that they believe the adolescent has a problem. ***(B)*** The parent challenges the adolescent to prove that they don't have a problem by agreeing to a certain set of principles. **(C)** If the adolescent does not have a problem, then the contract serves only to highlight that fact. ***(D)*** If the adolescent has a problem, over time they will experience the consequences of the contract.

The contract is actually a series of contracts. It should be structured in such a way that each time the adolescent fails to maintain the contract, another one is drawn up with greater consequences. Each contract progresses to a more restrictive set of limits and expectations. The goal is to maneuver the out of control adolescent into agreeing to go to counseling, to make constructive behavior changes, or face a loss of freedom or the ultimate consequence of not being allowed to live at home.

Parents need backbone. Don't attempt a contract until you are ready to follow through. If you don't have the ability to fulfill the contract and provide the consequences, the contract will not work. This may require you to go to counseling, assertiveness training, or to join a support group for parents with difficult adolescents.

Don't be afraid to seek professional help to regain control of your home or to work out realistic limits for your adolescent. Parenting an adolescent is not easy and you are not alone.

Limits and consequences are crucial to the contracting process. Behavior expectations and consequences must be age appropriate and should fit the behaviors or incidents in question. Don't make threats that you are unable or unwilling to back up. Remember, you need backbone. Consequences must be reasonable and enforceable.

Which of these examples is logical and reasonable?

EXAMPLE:

Behavior	16 y/o comes home one hour after curfew
Consequence	16 y/o comes home one hour earlier the next night they go out

EXAMPLE:

Behavior	15 y/o takes $5 that belongs to you
Consequence	15 y/o is grounded for two months

Timing is a critical issue in the contracting process. Goals need to be thought out and agreed to by both parents. Parents need to spend time discussing the expectations and agreeing to the consequences that will be used. If parents do not provide a united front when contracting, the contract will fail. This may mean that parents need to participate in counseling together to resolve parenting differences. When differences are worked out, then it is time to decide when the contract will be presented to the adolescent.

- ❑ Take advantage of a crisis situation with your adolescent to inform them that you are working on a contract so that both sides will have some agreeable rules to go by.
- ❑ Don't attempt to contract with your adolescent during an argument, when they are angry, or if they are high or intoxicated.
- ❑ Decide where the contract is to be presented. Pick a neutral location in the house to sit down and discuss the contract.
- ❑ Set aside a specific time to meet with your adolescent to discuss the contract.
- ❑ Make sure that there is plenty of time to discuss the contract and answer any questions that may arise during the discussion.
- ❑ Be flexible and ready to negotiate certain points of the contract. Your adolescent needs to have an investment in the contract to make it work.
- ❑ Know what points of the contract can be negotiated and which ones are not up for negotiation. Be as flexible as possible without backing down on your expectations.
- ❑ Prepare yourself for a confrontation and do not allow your adolescent to manipulate you into an argument.
- ❑ Appear cool and reasonable; remain as calm as possible.

Top line/Bottom line contracts are the most effective. The top line of the contract indicates that the adolescent is maintaining or exceeding expectations, and can handle more responsibility and freedom. The top line of the contract acts as incentive for the adolescent. Without some type of incentive, the contract is not attractive to the adolescent. The bottom line of the contract indicates that the adolescent is not maintaining the terms of the contract and that the consequences agreed to in the contract will be enforced. A contract needs to have both a top and bottom line.

Example:

> *TOP LINE* – If Bob maintains 9 out of 10 items on the contract for six weeks, his curfew will be moved from 10:30 p.m. until 11:30 p.m. on Friday and Saturday nights and a new contract will be negotiated.
>
> *BOTTOM LINE* – If Jill fails to maintain 8 of 12 items on the contract for six weeks, she will go see a drug counselor for an evaluation and follow the counselor's recommendations.

Point contracts are often the easiest to monitor and maintain. The behaviors and expectations, along with certain rules are each assigned a point value. Appropriate behavior is assigned a positive point value and inappropriate behavior is assigned a negative value.

☞ If the adolescent follows through with expectations, then they receive the points assigned to that task or behavior. If the adolescent fails to follow through with a task or responsibility, they receive a zero for the day.

☞ If the adolescent is involved in inappropriate behavior, the adolescent will receive the negative points assigned to that behavior. If they do not display that particular inappropriate behavior, they receive a zero for that day. *[See the sample point contract at the end of this chapter.]*

☞ The adolescent must then maintain a set number of points each week to meet the expectations of the contract. This works well because points can be added or subtracted on a daily basis and the adolescent can clearly see where they stand. This makes the adolescent and their behavior responsible for the consequences they experience, not you.

Example:

Chores:	Do dishes daily - earn 5 points each day Feed the dog - earn 2 points each day Keep room clean - earn 5 points each day
Behaviors:	Use of profanity - lose 5 points (a day) Violate curfew - lose 10 points (a day) Hitting sister - lose 25 points (a day)
Bottom Line:	Must maintain 80 points per week for four weeks or go to counseling
Top Line:	If you maintain 95 points per week for four weeks, then curfew extended 1 hour.

Setting the Top and Bottom line on a point contract:

The Top Line on a point contract should be set at 95% of all possible points the adolescent could earn in a week (if they follow through with every expectation and do not lose points for inappropriate behavior). We know that no adolescent is perfect and we cannot expect 100% compliance.

The formula for the Top Line is:

All possible points x .95 = Top Line

The Bottom Line on a point contract should be set at 80% of all possible points the adolescent could earn in a week (if they follow through with every expectation and do not lose points for inappropriate behavior). It is set at 80% of all possible points to make the contract fair and to give the adolescent a margin of error within which to work. Adolescents must be able to learn and grow from their mistakes.

The formula for the Bottom Line is:

All possible points x .80 = Bottom Line

Adolescent input is critical to the success of the contracting process. Adolescents cannot be forced into a contract, but need to be coaxed into the contract through involvement in the process. They need to feel that they are getting something out of the deal. If the top line of the contract is attractive, they will be quick to agree to the bottom line.

Once the contract has been established, sit back and monitor your adolescent's behavior in accordance with the terms of the agreement. Do not make daily announcements as to the status of the contract. This will promote conflict. Do not act as if you are out to get your adolescent. Let them fail or succeed with the contract on their own. This gives the contract the power and takes away your responsibility for your adolescent's behavior. If they cannot maintain the contract, it is their responsibility. This process helps break the denial, and takes away their ability to blame you for the problem.

Follow-up on the contract. If the bottom line of the contract is violated, it is important to follow up on it as soon as possible. If you do not follow up on the consequences in a short period of time, you are signaling to the adolescent that the contract is not important and has no power. The same holds true if the adolescent makes the top line of the contract. If the adolescent does not receive the reward they worked for, interest is lost and the contract is no longer an effective tool for managing behavior.

Set a time limit. The contract should have a time limit so the adolescent will know when it will be reviewed and re-negotiated. Adolescents lack the ability to put off rewards and punishment for extended periods of time. Make the review period reasonable. A period longer than three months is often not effective.

10 Points to an Effective Contract

Contracts need to contain:

- ☐ The date the contract is initiated.
- ☐ The date that the contract will be reviewed, renegotiated, or expire.
- ☐ The behaviors that are unacceptable.
- ☐ The rules and expectations.
- ☐ A top line – the point that will indicate that the adolescent is exceeding expectations, and can handle more responsiblity and freedom.
- ☐ A bottom line – the point that will indicate the contract has failed, the adolescent cannot handle responsibility and freedom, and consequences will be enforced.
- ☐ A method to monitor compliance or non-compliance
- ☐ Consequences clearly spelled out for specific behaviors or rule violations – and/or –
- ☐ Consequences for failure to maintain contract.
- ☐ Signatures of the parties involved to indicate their agreement to the terms.

Sample Contract

October 14, 1989

In the interest of creating a workable and liveable home environment between my son and myself, I would like to establish a few ground rules which I feel would inspire communication and promote family growth.

1. Most importantly that you follow through with counseling.

2. Would like very much to encourage that you attend church on Sunday.

3. I feel a curfew is mandatory in order to maintain structure in the family unit as a whole and should be observed at all times.

   Example: 9:00 p.m. on school nights
   11:00 p.m. on weekends

4. How many nights a week would depend strongly on the attitude and behavior prior to the night in question. Also that homework be completed before hand.

5. Smoking will be allowed in the house as long as it is restricted to the living room and kitchen. Violation will result in a discussed period of time without privileges.

6. Whatever the situation at hand, I will be more than willing to sit down sensibly and talk things out in a calm and collected manner. I will not tolerate cursing, swearing, or any type of violent outburst.

7. Your friends are allowed in the living room only, and are not allowed any smoking privileges within the house. There will be no overnight visits with friends at this time.

8. Maintaining a clean environment within the home. This would include personal hygiene and picking up your dirty clothes and putting them in the laundry. If you fix yourself something to eat, clean up the mess left behind. That your room be kept in an orderly manner.

9. Since I have given you smoking privileges at home, I feel there will be no need for you to smoke in school or on school grounds.

10. I'm willing to do my part in order to keep things in some sort of sensible order. We can work together as a family and keep the lines of communication open. I would like to ask that you do the same.

Please feel free to discuss any disagreements or questions about any of the rules. We will have to work together in order to accomplish a warm and loving structure in our home.

If these rules are agreeable to you, please sign the agreement in good faith towards working together.

Signature: ______________________________

Signature: ______________________________

Sample Contract Quiz

✎ The contract on the left was written for a 14-year-old boy. Look at the contract on the left and answer the following questions by circling your answer.

① Does the contract have a start and review date?

Yes No

② Are the behavior expectations and rules clearly spelled out?

Yes No

③ Are the consequences for rule violations or a contract violation clearly spelled out?

Yes No

④ Does the contract have a means to determine if the adolescent is exceeding the expectations of the contract and can handle more responsibility and freedom?

Yes No

⑤ Does the contract have a means to determine if the adolescent is not living up to the basic expectations of the contract and cannot handle reponsibility and freedom?

Yes No

⑥ Does the contract have a means to monitor compliance or noncompliance?

Yes No

⑦ Would you consider this to be a workable and enforceable contract?

Yes No

Sample Contract

1. **Unacceptable Behaviors:**

   Swearing and name calling
   Throwing things
   Broken curfew or rules
   Grades falling
   Lying
   Pounding on any objects
   Screaming and backtalk
   Chores not done
   Cutting classes

   Each week goes from Sunday through Saturday. If four or more behaviors appear within one week, Bob has seven days to correct the behaviors. if not corrected, the "what if plan" goes into effect.

2. Using or finding drug paraphernalia, the what if plan goes into effect immediately.
3. **WHAT IF PLAN:** Evaluation of chemical usage and treatment if recommended.
4. **Tasks and Responsibilities:**

   Vacuum living room - Thursday
   Garbage - Thursday
   Bedroom - Bed made and clothes off floor every day before noon
   Doors closed and locked when leaving house
   Allowance - $18 weekly given on Friday morning
   School lunches come out of allowance
   Consequences - $1 off allowance for each thing not done

5. **Expectations and Rules:**

   Curfew: 10:00 p.m. Sunday through Thursday; 12:00 Friday and Saturday
   If curfew is broken, Bob will stay home two extra nights the next week.

   Supper: Bob will be home for supper on the nights one or both parents are home to make supper. If supper is missed, Bob will stay home one extra night the next week.

   From Sunday through Thursday, Bob will be home three nights a week. Bob will be home either Friday or Saturday each week to spend an evening with the family. Being home in the evening means from supper time on.

   NO SMOKING IN HOUSE: If smoking, no cigarette butts on steps, in yard, or in driveway. Consequence $5 off next allowance.

   Bob will give phone numbers of his whereabouts for each evening he is out of the house. Consequence: will stay home two extra nights the next week.

   Follow household rules posted on refrigerator.

   No clothing left at other people's houses.

   Attend an A.A. or N.A. meeting weekly.

   Attend all after-care appointments.

6. **PRIVILEGES EARNED FOR FULFILLMENT OF CONTRACT:**

   Fulfillment means that there are no more than 15 broken rules or tasks in one month (numbers 4 and 5) and the what if plan has not had to be used.

At the end of one month, Bob will get to go on a special weekend outing. At the end of three months, if the contact has been fulfilled, we will be willing to re-negotiate.

Signature: ____

Date: ____________________________

Sample Contract Quiz

✎ The contract on the left was written for a 16-year-old boy. Look at the contract on the left and answer the following questions by circling your answer.

① Does the contract have a start and review date?

Yes No

② Are the behavior expectations and rules clearly spelled out?

Yes No

③ Are the consequences for rule violations or a contract violation clearly spelled out?

Yes No

④ Does the contract have a means to determine if the adolescent is exceeding the expectations of the contract and can handle more responsibility and freedom?

Yes No

⑤ Does the contract have a means to determine if the adolescent is not living up to the basic expectations of the contract and cannot handle reponsibility and freedom?

Yes No

⑥ Does the contract have a means to monitor compliance or noncompliance?

Yes No

⑦ Would you consider this to be a workable and enforceable contract?

Yes No

Pre-Contract Worksheet

Complete this worksheet and use it as a guide to building your contract.

Rules you would like your adolescent to follow.
1. Curfew is 10 p.m. Sunday thru Thursday 11 p.m. on Friday and Saturday
2. No smoking
3. No friends in the house when no one is home.
4. Cannot take the family car without permission
5. 20 minute time limit when using the phone

Responsibilities/Tasks you expect your adolescent to perform.
1. Take out garbage daily and cans to the curb on Thursday
2. Pickup room daily
3. Load dishwasher daily after supper
4. Mow the lawn every Saturday
5. Do the laundry every Saturday

Behaviors you consider to be inappropriate for your adolescent.
1. Stealing, taking, borrowing items without permission
2. Use of profanity, name calling or verbal abuse
3. Throwing or breaking things
4. Grabbing, pushing, or hitting brother or sister
5. Use of alcohol/drugs or being at parties with alcohol/drugs

Consequences you consider to be appropriate for broken rules, jobs not done, and inappropriate behaviors.
1. Decrease curfew by one hour or more/ grounding
2. Loss of telephone privileges
3. Loss of use of the car
4. Go to counseling and/or attend drug treatment program
5. Cannot live at home

Top Line (indicates the contract is working and provides incentives)

Bob has been asking for his curfew to be extended to midnight on Friday and Saturday Nights.

Bottom Line (indicates the contract is broken and provides consequences)

I want Bob to go to counseling to deal with his behavior and attitude.

Sample Contract

Today's Date: 6-16-90	Review/Expiration Date: 7-14-90	Week of: 6-16-90 Thru: 6-22-90

Responsibilities / Tasks	**Value + or -**	**SAT**	**SUN**	**MON**	**TUE**	**WED**	**THU**	**FRI**	**Total Points**
Take out garbage daily	+5	5	5	5	5	5	5	5	30
Garbage cans to curb / Thursday	+5						5		5
Pick up room daily	+5	5	0	5	5	5	0	5	25
Mow lawn on Saturday	+10	10							10
Attend all classes at school	+5			5	5	0	5	5	20
20 minute phone limit	+2	2	2	0	2	2	2	2	12
Behaviors / Rules	**Value + or -**	**SAT**	**SUN**	**MON**	**TUE**	**WED**	**THU**	**FRI**	**Total Points**
Curfew 10 p.m. Sun. - Thurs.	+10		10	10	10	10	0		40
Curfew 11 p.m. Fri. and Sat.	+10	10						10	20
Stealing / taking objects	-5	0	0	0	0	0	0	0	0
Profanity or verbal abuse	-5	-5	0	0	0	0	0	0	-5
Throwing / breaking objects	-10	0	0	0	0	-10	0	0	-10
Grabbing / hitting others	-10	0	0	0	0	0	0	0	0
Use of alcohol / drugs	-20	0	0	0	0	0	0	0	0
Total Points Possible	**194**	**Total Points for the Week**							**147**

Top Line (indicates the contract is working)

If Bob gets 184 points for 4 (four) weeks in a row, his curfew will be extended to midnight on Friday and Saturday and a new contract will be written.

Bottom Line (indicates the contract is broken)

Bob must maintain 155 points per week or Bob agrees to go to counseling and a new contract will be written.

Signature:	Signature:

Pre-Contract Worksheet

Complete this worksheet and use it as a guide to building your contract.

Rules you would like your adolescent to follow.

Responsibilities/Tasks you expect your adolescent to perform.

Behaviors you consider to be inappropriate for your adolescent.

Consequences you consider to be appropriate for broken rules, jobs not done, and inappropriate behaviors.

Top Line (indicates the contract is working and provides incentives)

Bottom Line (indicates the contract is broken and provides consequences)

Contract

Today's Date:	Review/Expiration Date:	Week of: Thru:

Responsibilities / Tasks	Value + or -	SAT	SUN	MON	TUE	WED	THU	FRI	Total Points
Behaviors / Rules	**Value + or -**	**SAT**	**SUN**	**MON**	**TUE**	**WED**	**THU**	**FRI**	**Total Points**
Total Points Possible		**Total Points for the Week**							

Top Line (indicates the contract is working)

Bottom Line (indicates the contract is broken)

Signature:	Signature:

A Possible Solution

A possible solution to the problems associated with an alcohol/drug abusing adolescent, may be to enroll them in a formal chemical abuse treatment program. Parents need to know that chemical abuse/dependency treatment centers following traditional standards promote the disease concept of chemical dependency.

The disease concept of chemical dependency holds that people who are experiencing chemical dependency have a progressive, chronic and fatal disease that has a set of observable and predictable symptoms. The prescription for arresting the disease is abstinence from alcohol/drug use; the person experiencing the disease is never cured.

It's very difficult for families to see chemical dependency as a disease. How can an adolescent who looks physically healthy and strong suffer from a disease? The treatment process can be marred by the parent's resistance to the disease concept. The struggle with the disease concept often times reinforces the denial system of the parent and the adolescent. But parents need not accept the disease concept for treatment to be successful.

If you are the parent of a chemically abusing adolescent, whether you believe that the adolescent is experiencing a disease process or not is irrelevant. The primary objective is to get that adolescent to stop abusing chemicals and to bring their behavior in line with socially accepted standards and expectations for an adolescent their age. The objective needs to be abstinence for the adolescent.

Chemical dependency treatment comes in many forms. Basic approaches to treating adolescents fit into one of three areas: outpatient treatment, short term inpatient hospitalization, and long term residential treatment. With each level, the structure of the treatment environment increases, becomes more restrictive. Many centers now integrate family therapy into the treatment plan.

The main goal of each approach is to help the adolescent and their family become aware of the impact chemicals and drug affected behavior has had on their lives. In the treatment process structure, accountability and experience help to shape the thinking of the adolescent. Adolescents lack mature thinking and the ability to cognitively integrate concepts into their frame of reference. Adolescents often demonstrate self centered thinking and behave as if the world revolves around them.

Adolescents can promise you the world, and often actually believe that they can deliver it to you. Unfortunately, their good intentions do not produce the behaviors that they promise. By providing them with firm clear consequences for inappropriate behavior, you help them experience a cause and effect relationship that will encourage them to get in touch with more positive thinking and behavior.

OUTPATIENT TREATMENT

Outpatient counseling takes place on a drop-in basis with self reporting by the adolescent. The family is the key to understanding the level of change that is taking place. The drawback to this approach is that the adolescent can become skilled in reporting the changes the counselor wants to hear. Without collateral information and monitoring through drug screens, the adolescent lacks accountability.

The outpatient treatment program approach is often an individual or group oriented experience which includes drug information/education sessions, individual counseling or group counseling with a number of abusing adolescents. The treatment group comes together to learn through an interactive process of self disclosure, trust and relationship building experiences that impact the adolescent and influence change. With individual or group counseling, the adolescent can learn to say the right thing for a day each week or for a couple of hours a day depending on the structure of the program.

INPATIENT TREATMENT

Inpatient treatment is more restrictive. The adolescent resides at the facility under 24 hour supervision. It combines elements of the outpatient program such as drug education and group therapy with the structure of a secure drug free environment. If the program is doing its job, the level of accountability should be higher with this treatment approach. Inpatient treatment programs can run from several days to several months.

LONG TERM RESIDENTIAL TREATMENT

Long term programs run from several months to a year or more depending on the needs of the adolescent and their level of maturation. Theoretically, these programs provide the greatest degree of accountability over a longer time span.

Long term treatment programs combine elements of outpatient and inpatient programs with a daily living regime that extends over a period of time to help the adolescent achieve lasting behavior change. Here, the adolescent is monitored for lasting behavior changes and does not have the ability to consistently manipulate the program.

Resource Worksheet

To find the adolescent treatment program in your local area, call the local hotline listed in the yellow pages, your city or county substance abuse or mental health agency, your local school, hospital, church or parents support group. To get a better idea of the services offered by a program talk with parents who have had a family member in the program.

If you are living with an acting out adolescent, you will want to find out the answer to the following questions . . .

✍ What are the adolescent treatment centers in my local area?

① ______________________ ② ______________________
Name | Name

______________________ ______________________
Address | Address

______________________ ______________________
Phone | Phone

✍ What are the problem areas that they specialize in?

① ______________________ ② ______________________

______________________ ______________________

______________________ ______________________

✍ What are the services offered for individual, group, family counseling, occupational therapy and recreational therapy?

① ______________________ ② ______________________

______________________ ______________________

______________________ ______________________

✍ What is the average length of involvement in the program?

① ______________________ ② ______________________

✍ What are the daily or total program costs?

① ______________________ ② ______________________

✍ What type of insurance or financing plans do they accept?

① ______________________ ② ______________________

______________________ ______________________

✍ What are the benefits on my health insurance plan for chemical dependency or mental health treatment?

____

____

____

✍ What is the deductible on my plan and what is my share of the treatment program cost?

____

____

____

✍ Miscellaneous Notes

____

____

____

____

____

____

Casualties of War

The following is a story of an adolescent caught up in alcohol/drug abuse . . .

Jackie's Story

I first started using when I was eleven years old. I was with a friend and she asked me if I wanted to drink a beer. I was scared because I had saw what it had done to my mom when she was drinking. When my mom was drinking, she was living with us, and it hurt me to see what she was doing with her life.

When sixth grade started, I was learning from my friends and I would do what they did. I drank a couple of times that year at movie parties. I was worried about what was going to happen when I left the party. I was also scared because if my dad caught me I probably would have gotten the 3rd degree and told that I was taking after my Mom.

The summer after my sixth grade year had come around and I had learned a lot from my drinking experiences during the school year and enjoyed the feeling of getting a buzz or getting drunk. That summer I drank about six times with my friends and it was a lot more fun than during the school year because my curfew was later and I wasn't worried about getting caught because my parents weren't home much.

During the seventh grade, I would say I was either going to a movie or else going to a friend's house to watch movies. Then, I would ask for some money to go to the movies or get movies and would use the money to get beer about twice a month. I would usually buy a six pack and drink about 3-5 beers. Then, I'd get sick and give the others away. I felt like crap after lying to my dad about going to the movies, but my friend usually solved that by saying, "Ah, don't worry about it they'll never find out what you're doing." I really felt I was using my parents to get money for the beer I didn't really need, but the beer that I wanted.

Then, at the end of that year, my drinking started to increase from 3-5 beers to just 5. That was the amount I could handle without getting sick. Then I started going to different parties, at the park or at somebody's house when the parents had left for the weekend. I felt it was the time of my life, until my dad asked me if I had been drinking. I still lied and felt bad about the way I was lying to him, but I felt I had to lie to keep on drinking for the summer and we had a lot of plans for getting drunk.

Then, the summer after the seventh grade, to start it out right, we had to have a out of school party. My dad was gone out of town and I said "hey, let's just have it at my house." Not too many people wanted to have it at my house, but it was a place to stay overnight and a place where you could get as drunk as you wanted to. Well, my dad had left and all I had to do was to break into the house and we were home free (that's what we thought anyway). After we broke in, we called someone who would buy for us. We had it all set up and the buyer had brought a case and a half of beer for six people and I had eight beers and never got sick, so I decided the next time I would drink I would have to see how many I could drink.

That summer, I also went to my mom's for her wedding. My dad called and asked if I had been in the house while he was gone, and after about three calls of bugging me about it, I finally admitted to it. I really felt I should have gotten into trouble but nothing happened, so I thought "well, I might as well drink if my mom really doesn't give a damn." So we went out camping the second night I was there and got bombed. I was puking all over the place and figured, "Ah, that's okay, nobody will care, I can drink out here if I want to." I went home (to my mom's) and nothing even happened. They just asked how it went and we all said it went great. We had a fun time. So the next week we went to a kegger and I had 6 - 16 oz. glasses of beer and two mixed drinks. Then I went back to the house and they asked how the movie was and I could barely stand up. Then I started to get sick and puked all over. All that came out of it was that I had to clean it up, so I knew I would like it there because now I could drink with her whenever I wanted. It really didn't make me feel good because I knew if I was home with my dad that he would have been very pissed off at me. I had drank quite a bit that summer and really felt bad for drinking all the time, and acting the way I did to my family and friends.

The eighth grade started out good with a back to school dance and I said to my friend "why don't we get drunk?" and she said "Yeah, lets!" So we found a buyer and got a 12 pack plus a couple and got really drunk. I was really paranoid at what the teachers would think when we walked in, but I never said a word, so I had a great time being wild until my counselor came up to me and asked if we were having a good time and we didn't talk, just nodded out heads. They looked at us like they knew what we had been doing. I was really scared and wanted to leave.

By December that year, my drinking had progressed from 4 to 5 times a month. I liked getting drunk more often than I used to. It was a great feeling of getting drunk or getting blasted. It took 6 to 7 beers to give me that same buzz now. I usually drank beer. When I had the money or when there was something going on like a dance, it would help me feel loose. I didn't know why I liked getting drunk except to hide feelings I had, or when I was pissed off, or when I wanted to feel more comfortable around other people.

The summer after my eighth grade, I went with my mom to St. Paul and to Georgia. When I went to St. Paul, my Mom would ask me if I wanted a beer and I said sure. Then she would make me hide it from Grandma. I felt like why should I be doing this, but just a couple won't hurt anything. So I kept on drinking when I went to Georgia for a wedding. They were drinking all of the time. They had kegger after kegger and I thought "wow, this is going to be great!" So the first night I had 6 or 7 glasses of beer and I was buzzing pretty good until I woke up the next morning. The second night I drank about 10 glasses of beer and went to the front of the house in my aunt's car and laid down until I puked up everything I had eaten that day. I really felt bad about puking. I apologized, but I felt that wasn't even close enough to making it up to them. Mom said, "It's okay, it's all cleaned up and it happens sometimes." She wasn't even mad. I felt that I should have at least got into a little trouble. Then, when I got back to my Dad's, everyone had gotten into pot. Some friends asked if I wanted to try some and I said sure, just as long as nobody finds out about it. So I took 2-3 hits and waited to feel something. I never did, so the next day I had 5 hits and was feeling better than getting drunk. I would have liked to smoke pot more often but I just started drinking again, and kept getting sick.

Ninth grade, I was drinking again, and more than I usually did. I drank every weekend and whenever I had money. I always got pissed when I didn't have any money. After a while I knew why. It was because I drank too much. I didn't get drunk until I found money or stole it from my Dad. Then I started to buy pot. I would buy as much as I could with the money I had. I usually bought an 1/8 oz. until I started running out of money, so I started stealing from the neighbors, and got caught. I felt like a real loser for having to steal, but I needed that money for my drugs. My using was unreal. I bought bag after bag. I didn't use every day, but every other day at least 2-3 times a day. I would be high every second of the day when I smoked pot. I would quit for two weeks, then smoke for a month and it kept going on like that. I really felt sorry for stealing the money for the pot, but at that time I really didn't care about anything, just pot.

✍ *(To better understand Jackie's alcohol/drug use, fill out this chart.)*

Grade	Chemical Used	Quantity	Frequency
6th Grade			
7th Grade			
8th Grade			
9th Grade			

When we were going to get a bag of pot, we would plan it all out, so nobody would know what we had planned. Then we would go to the park, and wait at the park till someone would drive by and get us some weed. Then we would be happy and excited. I couldn't wait till we got a hold of someone. All day I was in a good mood. We would either chip in and buy it or else I would just get a bag by myself and just give it away when somebody needed some or wanted some. I would hide my pot in lots of places that I didn't think anybody would look. First, it started out in my top dresser drawer. When I came to use more pot, I slit a hole in my teddy bear's arm and stuck it in the body of it. That was because I was always paranoid. I would sometimes hide it in the park, if I had a lot. I didn't know where else to put it when I was scared of getting caught.

I would tell my dad I was going to a movie or to someone's house to study, but instead used the money to buy weed or alcohol. If my eyes were red, I would make up some excuses like I was crying or else I got soap in my eyes. I really felt bad lying to him, but I had to protect my using. We never talked about drugs much until he suspected that I had been using. Then I would leave the house and wouldn't come back till I wanted. I felt nervous about his knowing I was using and had to run from the truth and my feelings. I had to have pot at parties and movies, or when just running around and having fun. I felt I needed pot to make me feel wanted or accepted by my friends or some of the people I hung around with. I usually felt good when I was using unless I puked or got in fights with friends or boyfriends. I had to be cool so that wouldn't bother me then until later when I found out what I had really done. I used to think about getting high all the time. Friday was usually the day I would get a bag, or a couple of joints. I was really happy that Friday after school. I had the connections and would be ready to go, except I had to make an excuse to my dad and sometimes that wasn't too easy. I would do almost anything to get some pot. I tried to quit but I needed to get high.

✍ What were the excuses Jackie used to cover her alcohol/drug use?

____

____

____

____

____

____

✍ Why did Jackie feel she needed alcohol/drugs?

____

____

____

✍ What were the hiding places Jackie used to stash her alcohol/drug supply?

____

____

____

____

When I was at a party, I would say "Oh not tonight, I have to go home early." It would only last for awhile, then I would say, "I'm only going to catch a little buzz" and I would get really high. Then I would say "after this joint or bag, I'll quit." I would last two weeks and then there would be a dance going on so I would have to get high again. I felt like crap because I told people I would quit and never did. I felt sorry for them not being able to trust me anymore. Then I would say "I am going to save a joint or a bowl" and I would end up smoking it right after saying that. I felt good at the time but I kept going back on my word. I didn't feel good being who I was.

I would say "I won't get stoned just catch a buzz", but ended up smoking a whole bowl. It was great until I got home. Then I became paranoid and was scared of getting caught.

✍ How did Jackie attempt to cut down or control her alcohol/drug useage?

____

____

____

____

____

Also when I would use, I got very destructive and wanted to fight and get all my anger out. I would say things to my friends like "I don't need you or anybody else on my back, just leave me alone." I would say "get the hell out of my life". What was scary was that I needed my friends. I felt like total crap after I said that because my friends mean so much to me. I felt worried about what they might think. When I would get drunk and pissed off, I would always find something to punch just to get out my anger. It hurt, but made me feel better.

I was in one accident when smoking pot. We swerved into the ditch and hit a fence post. Not much happened except a little dent in the front bumper. I was more scared than anything.

I thought about suicide a couple of times, but only planned out one of them. I planned to go in the garage and start the car and suffocate of carbon monoxide poisoning. Then I figured I had more to live for and I felt bad about wanting to kill myself.

✍ What kind of problems did Jackie experience when she used alcohol/drugs?

____

____

____

____

My value system has really changed since I have been using. First I've lost all trust from family and friends. I've lied to them so much they really don't know whether to trust me or not. I feel I've hurt all of them very much.

The friendship between family and friends has changed a lot too. I can't sit down and be able to talk about feelings. I feel we've been separated and have lost all interest in each other. I've lost interest in church and church activities. I didn't want to go to church or Sunday school and sometimes I would skip confirmation. I lost interest in school work and school. I felt that it was just a place to waste time and get bossed around.

I lost interest in basketball and volleyball. I wanted to get high instead of wasting my time doing something I liked. I really missed volleyball and wish I would have stayed out for it. I felt bad because I didn't believe in myself.

I lost all responsibility in everything. I never followed through on anything. I didn't do my jobs, work around the house or anything to help out. I felt left out and alienated. It made me feel very lonely.

It hurt my dad because we could talk together and we were always close and now we can't talk and we've drifted away from each other. It hurts to see how close we were and now it'ts like we're not even friends.

I hurt my brother because he didn't want to believe what I was doing, so I kept lying and we never talked about it. It made me feel bad that I couldn't tell him the truth. It hurt my brother a lot because we were so close before I started using and now we don't do anything together. It really hurts me to see where our relationship is going. We always talked and now we can't because I wanted to use instead of being with my brother. I feel guilty for just leaving him there in the dust and not even really caring about him or any of my family members.

✍ What effects did alcohol/drug use have on Jackie's value system?

____

____

____

____

____

✍ What happened to Jackie's relationships with people who were close to her as a result of her alcohol/drug use?

____

____

____

____

I lost a lot of money when I was using that could have helped me buy a lot of nice things, clothes especially. I probably could have bought a new wardrobe or bike. It really makes me stop and think, when I see what I lost.

It affected my school work. I couldn't think because most of the time I was high. My grades dropped and I didn't finish assignments that would have helped me get better grades. I feel I can get average grades but when I'm using I really don't even care.

I dropped out of a lot of sports too and that has really hurt me a lot. I don't think I could live without some kind of sport in my life. It hurts me to see I could be good at certain sports and not even try out for them.

Using has also affected my relationships with family, relatives, friends, teachers and pastor. It scares me to see our good relationships going down the tube when they used to be so good and complex. It hurts me to see how much trust has been lost by my using. I could talk to almost any of these people when I wasn't using. Now it's even hard to look them in the eye, because of everything I have lost, trust, good relationships, talking and sharing feelings. It scares me that someday I'll have to look everyone in the eye again. But it was hard for me to talk to anyone because it seemed like I was nothing to them, and now I know they really do care about me.

I lost a lot of freedom when I used because I broke so many of the rules. But that didn't stop me from doing what I wanted to. Then it came down to the cops chasing me and getting my driver's license taken away from me. My dad would try anything that would stop me for a while. I felt guilty for making my dad go through hell like he did. But it was hard for me to show or tell him so I always ran from the problem, which made me feel about two inches tall.

I didn't have much self-esteem or self confidence. The only way I would even try something was when I could be the best. And if I wasn't the best, I lost all interest in even trying for it. I thought I was doing the right thing. Now, I know it was the dumbest thing I could have done. I didn't feel good about myself at all because I wasn't good enough for me. That hurt my feeling good about myself as a person.

✍ What did Jackie lose as a result of her alcohol/drug use?

____

____

____

____

____

It was my dad that got me into treatment. He told me that I needed help and was going to have me see a counselor at the hospital near my house. I ran away before he could take me there. I didn't get far as my dad signed papers and had me picked up by the sheriff and brought to the treatment center. At first, I was angry about being in treatment but my group helped me realize how out of control I really was. Thanks dad!

Glossary

Glossary of Terms

Acid – slang term for LSD (lysergic acid) also called blotter, purple haze, or window pane. *(see LSD)*

Amobarbitol – a member of the barbiturate class of drugs that depress the central nervous system producing a sedative or hypnotic effect. *(see barbiturate)*

Amphetamines – a class of drugs that act to stimulate the central nervous system. Goes by street names of speed, beans, uppers, bennies, or black beauties.

Anesthetic – any chemical agent that causes insensitivity to pain or unconsciousness.

Angel Dust – Phencyclidine, is better known as PCP. A non-narcotic anesthetic agent that can produce serious adverse behavior reactions. *(see PCP)*

Anoxia – a condition consisting of a lack of oxygen in the body. Prolonged anoxia leads to brain damage, coma, and if not reversed, death.

Artillery – hypodermic needle or needle and accessories necessary to inject a drug.

Bad Trip – a bad experience from taking a drug. Usually associated with LSD, or other members of the hallucinogen class.

Bag – a quantity of drugs. Often associated with marijuana which when sold in one ounce quantities comes in a plastic sandwich bag.

Barbiturates – a class of drugs that have a sedative or hypnotic effect on the central nervous system. Street names include reds, yellow jackets, barbs, and downers.

Barbs – also called reds, downers, and yellow jackets. *(see barbiturates)*

Bat – a small baseball bat shaped brass pipe used for smoking marijuana one hit at a time, also called a pinch hitter, one hit, hooter, tooter or a oney.

Beam Me Up – a slang term meaning "get me high", usually associated with crack but can be used for other drugs. *(see crack)*

Beans – slang term for amphetamines, also called bennies, speed, uppers. *(see amphetamine)*

Bennies – slang term for Benzadrine or amphetamines, also called speed, uppers, or beans. *(see amphetamine)*

Binge – an extended period of drug useage that lasts at least 18 to 24 hours and can extend several days to several weeks. The user is in a drugged state from the beginning to the end of the binge period.

Black Beauties – Amphetamines named for their jet black color, also called speed, uppers, bennies, or beans. *(see amphetamine)*

Blasted – to be in a state of intoxication, high on drugs, also smashed, wasted, blown away, ripped, fried. *(see intoxication)*

Blotter – slang term for LSD. This form of LSD comes in the form of a very small square piece of paper (approximately $^1/_4$" x $^1/_4$") with a drop of the chemical on it, thus giving it ts name. *(see LSD)*

Blow – slang for cocaine, also to smoke marijuana. *(see cocaine, or maijuana)*

Blue Devil – capsule form of LSD, also can be amobarbitol. *(see LSD, or amobarbitol)*

Bong – a water pipe used in smoking marijuana, hashish, and cocaine. The pipe concentrates the smoke allowing the user to get a quicker more intense high. *(see marijuana, hashish, or cocaine)*

Bowl – slang term for a pipe, or pipe load of drugs, often used to refer to a pipe load of marijuana. *(see marijuana)*

Burned – to get cheated on a drug deal, buying a poor quality or substitute drug, same as ripped off. *(see ripped off)*

Burnout – is a slang term for a person who shows physical, intellectual, and/or emotional deterioration from drug use, also called a fry-baby, or crispy critter.

Busted – to be found out, or to be caught or arrested for illegal activity, may also refer to being out of money.

Buttons – slang term for peyote, and can also be associated with psilocybe mushrooms. *(see peyote, or psilocybin)*

Buzz – term that signifies the excitement and euphoria brought on by ingesting a mind altering chemical. *(see euphoria)*

Candy – slang term for barbiturates, can also be used to describe cocaine, also called nose candy. *(see cocaine)*

Cannabis Sativa – botanical (scientific) name for marijuana. *(see marijuana)*

Central Nervous System – the portion of the nervous system consisting of the brain and the spinal cord that controls activity. Mind altering drugs affect this portion of the body.

Christmas Trees – slang term for amphetamines, sold in tablet or capsule form. *(see amphetamine)*

Cocaine – a narcotic alkaloid that is extracted from coca leaves and is used as an anesthetic. Can be injected, snorted or smoked to produce the desired effects.

Coke – slang term for cocaine. *(see cocaine)*

Coke Head – a person who uses cocaine on a frequent basis and indicates it is their drug of choice. *(see cocaine)*

Cold Turkey – to withdraw from drugs by abruptly stopping useage, to withdraw without the aid of medications. *(see crash)*

Columbian – slang term for a high grade marijuana that is grown in and imported from the country of Columbia. *(see marijuana)*

Connect – to make a buy from a drug dealer.

Connection – a drug dealer or supplier.

Cook – to heat a drug to liquefy it, or the process of manufacturing a drug.

Cooker – a spoon or bottle cap used for heating a drug to liquefy the drug for injection. Also can refer to a person who manufactures an illegal drug.

Cop – slang term meaning to buy or obtain a drug, also used to refer to getting high, or to refer to a police officer. "I am going to cop a bag, cop a buzz, and try not to get caught by a cop."

Cotton Mouth – slang term for a dry mouth brought on as a side effect of ingesting a particular drug. Most often associated with smoking marijuana. *(see marijuana)*

Crack – a smokeable, solid, relatively pure and potent form of cocaine, also called rock. *(see cocaine)*

Crack Hag – a female addicted to crack who is selling sexual favors to obtain the drug. *(see crack)*

Crank – slang term for methamphetamine. Crank usually refers to the snorted (inhaled nasally) form of methamphetamine. *(see methamphetamine)*

Crispy critter – is a slang term for a person who shows physical intellectual, and/or emotional deterioration from drug use, also called a fry-baby, or burnout.

Croak – a mixture of crack and regular cocaine that is smoked to produce an intense euphoria.

Crystal – term for methamphetamine, a member of the stimulant class of drugs. *(see methamphetamine)*

Cut – to dilute a drug by adding foreign compounds to increase the quantity of the drug and thus increase profits. Milk sugar is often used to cut cocaine.

Delirium – temporary mental confusion and clouded state of consciousness that can result from intoxication and is characterized by anxiety, delusions, tremors, and hallucinations. *(see intoxication, or hallucinations)*

Delirium Tremons – is defined as a condition of acute delirium as the result of alcohol poisoning or alcohol withdrawal in alcoholics. *(see delirium)*

Delusion – a false belief that is firmly held in spite of factual information to the contrary. Drug abusers may experience delusions with repeated chemical use.

Dexies – slang term for dexadrine, a member of the stimulant class of drugs. *(see amphetamines)*

Dime Bag – a quantity of drugs costing ten dollars, usually associated with marijuana. *(see marijuana)*

Dirt Weed – a very low quality marijuana which produces little or no effect for the user when smoked, also called ditch weed, or skunk weed. *(see marijuana)*

Ditch Weed – see dirt weed and marijuana.

Dollies – slang term for methadone, a member of the narcotic class of drugs. *(see methadone, or narcotic)*

Doobie – slang term for marijuana cigarette, also called a joint. *(see marijuana)*

Dope – term for drugs found on the street, can also refer to marijuana. *(see marijuana)*

Downs – or downers, refers to the class of drugs that include barbiturates or tranquilizers. *(see barbs, or barbiturates)*

Drop – refers to the act of taking a drug orally, and is most often associated with taking LSD. *(see LSD)*

Drug Psychosis – a drug induced state of mental disorder that is marked by a deterioration of intellectual and social functioning, and a partial or complete withdrawal from reality.

Dry – to be without a supply of drugs, or the money to buy drugs, also to be without chemicals in the body.

Dugout – a wooden carrying case that has a hollow chamber to hold a small quantity of marijuana and a second small hollow chamber for housing a one hitter. *(see one hitter, or marijuana)*

Ecstasy – street name for the synthetic drug MDMA, first synthesized in 1914 and not widely used until approximately ten years ago. The drug is fast acting and has short lived effects. *(see MDMA)*

Eighth – a quantity of marijuana weighing one-eighth of an ounce. Expensive marijuana is sold in small quantities making it available to the average user. *(see marijuana)*

Fix – refers to an injection of drugs such as heroin or other opiates, can also refer to a dose of a particular drug. *(see heroin, or opiates)*

Flashback – a reoccurence of a previous drug taking experience, where the user feels the psychological and emotional effects of the drug without actually taking the drug. Most often associated with LSD or other hallucinogens. *(see LSD, or hallucinogens)*

Freeze – a smokeable form of methamphetamine that comes in a crystal form that resembles rock candy, also called ice, glass, or quartz. *(see methamphetamine)*

Freakout – a serious negative psychological and emotional experience from taking a drug. Causes the user to feel stress, paranoia, feelings of distortion, and may include feelings of depersonalization. Often associated with drugs that produce hallucinations such as LSD or other members of the hallucinogen family. *(see LSD, or hallucinogens)*

Freebase – a term to describe smoking cocaine, or a term for cocaine sulfate - a smokeable form of cocaine created by dissolving cocaine in an alkaline solution. *(see cocaine)*

Fry-Baby – is a slang term for a person who shows physical, intellectual, and/or emotional deterioration from drug use, also called a burnout, or crispy critter.

Glass – a smokeable form of methamphetamine that comes in a crystal form which resembles rock candy, also called ice, quartz, or freeze. *(see methamphetamine)*

Goofballs – slang term for barbiturates. *(see barbiturates, or barbs)*

Grass – slang term for marijuana. *(see marijuana)*

Hallucinations – a false sense of reality, objects or events, an altered state of reality that can be created by ingesting mind altering drugs such as LSD or peyote. *(see LSD, or peyote)*

Hallucinogens – family of drugs that produce a sense of altered reality and hallucinations, such as LSD, peyote, psilocybe mushrooms. *(see LSD, peyote, psyilocybin, or hallucinations)*

Hash – or hashish, a concentrated form of plant resin from the cannabis sativa plant, containing high amounts of THC the active ingredient in marijuana. *(see marijuana)*

Hawaiian – a high grade of marijuana that is grown in and imported from the state of Hawaii. *(see marijuana)*

Head – a person who is a frequent or consistent drug user. The user may be referred to as a pot head, or an acid head which indicates their drug of choice. *(see burnout)*

Headshop – a store that sells drug paraphernalia such as pipes, bongs, incense, magazines, or material that promotes the use of drugs.

Heart Palpitations – irregular and rapid beating of the heart, can be brought on by the use of drugs such as cocaine. *(see cocaine)*

Herb – slang term for marijuana. *(see marijuana)*

Heroin – a narcotic drug that is a member of the opiate family. *(see opiate, or narcotic)*

Hit – slang term to describe a dose of a drug, or an injection of a drug, also to take a drag off a marijuana cigarette. *(see marijuana)*

Homegrown – a locally grown variety of marijuana that is known for low potency. Growers have begun to develop potent strains of homegrown marijuana called sinsemilia. *(see marijuana, sinsemilia, ditch weed, dirt weed or skunk weed)*

Hooked – to be addicted to drugs, refers primarily to heroin. *(see heroin)*

Hooter – a small baseball shaped brass pipe used for smoking marijuana one hit at a time, also called a bat, pinch hitter, tooter, oney, or a one hitter.

Horse – slang term for heroin. *(see heroin)*

Huff – slang term that refers to inhalant drugs. Also may refer to the act of inhaling a solvent to produce a state of euphoria. *(see inhalant, or huffer)*

Huffer – slang term that refers to someone who uses inhalant drugs as their primary drug of choice. *(see inhalant, or huff)*

Hype – a hypodermic needle, also a slang term for a heroin addict. *(see heroin)*

Ice – a smokeable form of methamphetamine that comes in a crystal form, and resembles rock candy, also called glass, quartz, or freeze. *(see methamphetamine)*

Inhalant – any chemical substance that produces a vapor that can be inhaled to produce a feeling of euphoria. Chemical substances that are most often inhaled are solvents, cleaning fluids, and glues. *(see huff, or huffer)*

Intoxication – to induce through the ingestion of a chemical substance any of a series of states that range from euphoria and excitement to stupefaction.

Jamaican – a high grade of marijuana that is grown in and imported from the country of Jamaica. *(see marijuana)*

Joint – a marijuana cigarette. *(see marijuana)*

Junk – slang term for heroin, also can refer to other drugs. *(see dope)*

Junkie – refers to an opiate addict, can also refer to other drug addicts as the language becomes more generic. *(see opiate)*

Kilo – or kilogram, referring to 2.2 lbs. of a drug.

Laughing Gas – nitrous oxide, a gas associated with dentistry that produces mild euphoria.

Lethargy – an unconscious condition that resembles sleep. The individual can be aroused, but when left alone will fall back into this state of being.

Lid – a quantity of marijuana often weighing one ounce. *(see marijuana)*

Line – drugs, such as cocaine, that are snorted are often stretched out on a flat clean surface in a line, to make snorting easier. *(see cocaine)*

Locoweed – slang term for marijuana. *(see marijuana)*

Look A Likes – drugs that are legal but manufactured to look like an illegal drug. Often amphetamine look a like drugs are made of caffeine and can be sold legally, or on the black market as illegal drugs bringing higher prices and greater profits.

LSD – lysergic acid diethylamide is derived from the ergot fungus and was first snythesized in 1938. LSD is a member of the hallucinogen family and produces hallucinations within the user.

Ludes – methaqualone, a powerful and highly addictive depressant drug.

Mainline – to inject a drug directly into a vein or artery.

Marijuana – botanical name is cannabis sativa. A plant that grows wild, whose leaves and flower tops when dried and smoked produce a mind altering euphoria. The active ingredient is delta 9 tetrahydracannabinol. Marijuana can also be eaten or made into tea to produce euphoria.

Mary Jane – slang term for marijuana. *(see marijuana)*

MDMA – the synthetic drug 3, 4-methylenedioxymethamphetamine was first synthesized in 1914 as an appetite suppressant, and has hallucinogenic and amphetamine type qualities. The drug is linked to brain damage through research.

Mescaline – or mesc, an alkaloid drug that produces hallucinations and psychedelic effects.

Methamphetamine – a class of drugs that act to stimulate the central nervous system. Go by street names of meth, crystal, crank, speed, or black beauties.

Meth – slang term for methamphetamines. *(see methamphetamines)*

Methadone – (methadone hydrochloride) an organic compound that is used as an analgesic and in the treatment of heroin addiction. Heroin addicts are given methadone to prevent them from experiencing unpleasant withdrawl symptoms. Methadone itself is an addictive drug.

Miss Emma – slang term for morphine. *(see morphine)*

Morphine – an organic compound extracted from opium, used as an anesthetic or sedative in medicine. Repeated use produces addiction

Munchies – a state of ravenous appetite brought on as a side effect of smoking marijuana. *(see marijuana)*

Narcotic – a class of drugs that dulls the senses, reduces pain, and induces a dreamlike state or stupor. Drugs included in this class of drugs are opium, heroin, morphine, and methadone. Narcotic drugs are highly addictive.

Natural drug – a drug found in nature, that can be taken as is.

Nose candy – slang term for cocaine. *(see cocaine)*

One hitter – a small baseball shaped brass pipe used for smoking marijuana one hit at a time, also called a bat, pinch hitter, oney, or a hooter.

Oney – see one hitter.

Opium – drug prepared from the opium poppy containing alkaloids such as morphine, and codeine, also the base for heroin, a member of the narcotic family. *(see narcotic)*

Panama Red – a high grade of marijuana that is grown in and imported from the country of Panama. *(see marijuana)*

Paper – a small square of paper measuring several inches, used to hold a gram or less of a chemical substance such as cocaine. The paper is folded in such a way to make it a neat leak proof package.

Papers – cigarette paper used to roll marijuana to make a joint for smoking. *(see cannabis, or joint)*

PCP – Phencyclidine is better known as angel dust. A non-narcotic anesthetic agent that can produce serious adverse behavioral reactions – a member of the hallucinogen family. *(see angel dust)*

Physical Dependence – the body's growing dependence on the presence of a drug to maintain a specific level of physical functioning. When the physical self is denied the drug, the body goes through a period of re-adjustment (withdrawal) as the body attempts to compensate for the loss of the drug. *(see withdrawal)*

Pinch Hitter – a small baseball shaped brass pipe used for smoking marijuana one hit at a time, also called a bat, oney, hooter, or a one hitter.

Pink Hearts – an amphetamine that is pink in color and is formed in the shape of a heart. *(see amphetamine)*

Popped – slang term that refers to being arrested or caught. May also refer to the act of taking a drug.

Pot – slang term for marijuana. *(see marijuana)*

Psilocybin – a hallucinogen that is found in psilocybe mushrooms, produces hallucinations and psychedelic effects much like LSD. *(see LSD)*

Psychological Dependence – an individual who is psychologically dependent on a drug has a strong emotional desire to continue taking the drug because it helps them to cope emotionally.

Psychosis – a state of mental disorder that is marked by a deterioration of intellectual and social functioning. A partial or complete withdrawal from reality may be brought on by the use of this drug.

Purple Haze – a slang term for LSD. This form of LSD comes in a very small purple pellet which contains the chemical, thus giving it it's name. *(see LSD)*

Quarter – a quantity of marijuana weighing one-quarter of an ounce. Expensive marijuana is sold in smaller quantities making it available to the average user.

Quartz – a smokeable form of methamphetamine that comes in a crystal form that resembles rock candy, also called ice, glass, or freeze. *(see methamphetamine)*

Reds – slang term for barbiturates. *(see barbiturates, or barbs)*

Ripped Off – to get cheated on a drug deal, buying a poor quality or substitute drug. Same as burned. *(see burned)*

Roach – the butt of a marijuana cigarette. *(see marijuana)*

Roachclip – a device for holding the small butt of a marijuana cigarette so that the entire cigarette can be consumed without the user burning their fingers. *(see roach, also marijuana)*

Rock – a smokeable, solid, relatively pure and potent form of cocaine, also called crack. *(see cocaine)*

Rush – amyl nitrite or butyl nitrite that are abused as inhalants and produce a short lived high. Sold as rush or locker room. May also be a slang term indicating a sudden feeling of excitement and agitation.

Score – to make a drug deal, to get the drugs.

Semi-Synthetic Drugs – drugs that are found in nature and then processed in a laboratory to remove impurities and increase potency.

Shrooms – slang term for hallucinogenic mushrooms known as psilicybe mushrooms. *(see psilocybin)*

Sinsemilia – a seedless high grade marijuana which is best known for its intense long lasting high. *(see marijuana)*

Skunk Weed – a very low quality marijuana which produces little or no effect for the user when smoked. Also called dirt weed, or ditch weed. The slang term skunk can also denote a very high grade potent variety of marijuana. *(see marijuana)*

Smack – street name for heroin. *(see heroin, or opiate)*

Smoke Me Up – slang term referring to a user being given marijuana to get high. May also be a request on the part of the user to get high. *(see marijuana)*

Smoke Out – slang term referring to smoking large quantities of marijuana over an extended period of time. May also refer to a marijuana party. *(see marijuana)*

Snort – to ingest a powder form of a drug by inhaling it through the nostrils. Cocaine is often taken in this fashion. *(see cocaine)*

Snow – slang term for cocaine. *(see cocaine)*

Solvent – a liquid that is used to dissolve a substance, such as a cleaning solvent or stain remover. Most solvents produce a vapor that can be inhaled to produce a feeling of euphoria. *(see inhalant)*

Speed – slang term for amphetamines, also called beans, pink hearts, uppers, bennies, or black beauties. *(see amphetamines)*

Speedballs – a mixture of cocaine and heroin that is most often injected. *(see cocaine, or heroin)*

Strung Out – slang term used to refer to emotional or physical exhaustion that accompanies continuous heavy drug use.

Synthetic Drug – a drug that is manufactured in the laboratory with man made ingredients.

THC – delta 9 tetrahydracannabinol, the active ingredient in marijuana that produces a feeling of excitement and euphoria in the user. *(see marijuana)*

Tolerance – the ability of the body to absorb a drug on a continuous basis or in larger amounts without adverse effects.

Toot – slang term for cocaine, also can mean a hit. *(see cocaine, or hit)*

Tooter – a small baseball shaped brass pipe used for smoking marijuana one hit at a time, also called a pinch hitter, a bat, oney, hooter, or a one hitter. Term can also mean a straw or other small tubular device used for snorting cocaine. *(see cocaine)*

Tranks – slang term for tranquilizer or depressant drug. *(see barbiturate, or barbs)*

Trip – slang term for a drug taking experience involving hallucinogenic drugs, most often referring to LSD. *(see hallucinogen, or LSD)*

Window Pane – a slang term for LSD. This form of LSD consists of a very small see-thru square of hardened gelatin with the chemical in it, thus giving it it's name. *(see LSD)*

Withdrawal – the nervous system's response to the lack of a drug after physical dependence has occurred. The process is usually marked by physical and mental distress. Depending on the drug used, symptoms may range from fatigue and tremors, to coma and death. *(see physical dependence)*

Yellow Jackets – slang term for barbiturates or depressant drugs. *(see barbiturates, or barbs)*

Appendix

Answers

Unit Review - I.

Answers: 1. B 2. A 3. D 4. A 5. A 6. B 7. C 8. B

Unit Review - II.

Answers: 1. B 2. C 3. C 4. D 5. A 6. A 7. B 8. C

Unit Review - III.

Answers: 1. B 2. A 3. D 4. B 5. D 6. C 7. B 8. B

Unit Review - IV.

Answers: 1. D 2. C 3. A 4. B 5. A 6. D 7. A

Unit Review – V.

Answers: 1. C 2. A 3. B 4. B 5. D 6. B 7. D

Make The Match

Answers: 1. C 2. H 3. G 4. B 5. K 6. A
7. F 8. E 9. D 10. J 11. I

Support Groups

To find support groups in your local area, call your local hotline listed in the yellow pages, your city or county substance abuse or mental health agency, or look for listings in your local newspaper. If you do not find a support group in your area, or want more information on a particular support group, write to the organizations listed below.

Support Groups for families and relatives who are concerned about an adolescent's alcohol/drug use or related behavior problems:

Families Anonymous
P.O. Box 528
Van Nuys, CA 91408

Toughlove
P.O. Box 1069
Doylestown, PA 18901

12 Step Support Groups for substance abuse problems:

Alcoholics Anonymous
Box 459
Grand Central Station
New York, NY 10017

Narcotics Anonymous
World Service Office, Inc.
P.O. Box 9999
Van Nuys, CA 91409

For more information on substance abuse:

The American Council
for Drug Education
204 Monroe Street
Rockville, MD 20850

National Council
on Alcoholism
12 West 21st Street
New York, NY 10010

National Institute on Alcohol
Abuse and Alcoholism
National Institute on Drug Abuse
5600 Fishers Lane
Rockville, MD 20852

National Clearinghouse
for Drug Abuse Information
P.O. Box 1701
Washington, DC 20013

For more information on Mental Health issues such as suicide, depression, etc.:

National Mental Health Association
1021 Prince Street
Alexandria, VA 22314

National Alliance for the Mentally Ill
P.O. Box NAMI-AL
Arlington, VA 22216

For more information on Learning Disabilities:

Learning Disability Association of America
4156 Library Road
Pittsburgh, PA 15234

For more information on Eating Disorders:

American Anorexia/Bulimia
Association, Inc. (AA/BA)
133 Cedar Lane
Teaneck, NJ 07666

Anorexia Nervosa and Related
Eating Disorders, Inc. (ANRED)
P.O. Box 5102
Eugene, OR 97405

Suggested Reading

Choices and Consequences by Dick Schaefer. Minneapolis, MN: Johnson Institute Books, 1987.

Coping with Drug Abuse: A Lifeline for Parents by Joe Baker. Rockville, IL: DARE, Inc., 1982.

Custody by Tom Alibrandi. Los Angeles, CA: Pinnacle Books, 1979.

Loosening the Grip by Jean Kinney and Gwen Leaton. St. Louis: C.V. Mosby Company, 1983.

Toughlove: A Self-help Manual for Parents with Kids in Trouble by Phyllis and David York. Sellersville, PA: Community Service Foundation.

When It's Your Kid! by Glen O. Bair, Charlotte Elder and Phill Wallsmith. Kansas City: Lowell Press, 1978.

Your Perfect Right by Robert Alberti and Michael Emmons. San Luis Obispo, CA: Impact Publishers, 1986.

Resources

Adler, Israel and Kandel, Denise. *Cross-Cultural Perspectives on Developmental Stages in Adolescent Drug Use.* **Journal of Studies on Alcohol**. 1981, Volume 42, No. 9.

Bratter, Thomas E. and Forrest, Gary. ***Alcoholism and Substance Abuse: Strategies for Clinical Intervention***. The Free Press, New York: 1985.

Cohen, Sidney. *The Pharmacology of Alcohol.* **Postgraduate Medicine**. December 1978, Volume 6, No. 6

Consultation with National Institute on Drug Abuse. 5600 Fishers Lane, Rockville, Maryland 20857.

Davies, Bruce and Thomas, Geoffrey. ***Science and Sporting Performance: Management or Manipulation?***. Clarendon Press, Oxford: 1982.

Donovan, John and Jessor, Richard. *Problem Drinking and the Dimension of Involvement with Drugs: A Guttman Scalogram Analysis of Adolescent Drug Use.* **American Journal of Public Health**. May 1983, Vol. 73, No. 5

Finkelhor, David. ***Child Sexual Abuse***. The Free Press, New York: 1984.

Furst, Peter. ***Hallucinogens and Culture***. Chandler and Sharp Publishers, San Francisco: 1976.

Geller, Anne. *The Social, Psychological and Medical Management of Intoxication.* **Journal of Substance Abuse Treatment**, 1984, Volume 1.

Goldstein, Sam and Goldstein, Michael. **Managing Attention Disorders in Children**. John Wiley & Sons, New York: 1990.

Greer, James. *Adolescent Abuse of Typewriter Fluid.* **Southern Medical Journal**, March 1984, Volume 77, No. 3.

Griffith, H. Winter. ***Complete Guide to Prescription and Non-Prescription Drugs***. The Body Press, 1989.

Harrison, G. Pope and Hudson, James. ***New Hope for Binge Eaters***. Harper Colophon Books, New York: 1984.

Harwood, Henrick. *The Cost of Alcohol Abuse and Associated Injuries.* **Public Health Reports**, November-December 1987, Volume 102, No. 6.

Jellinek, E.M. ***Disease Concept of Alcoholism***. College and University Press, New Haven: 1960.

Johnson, Vernon. ***I'll Quit Tomorrow***. Harper and Row, San Francisco: 1980.

Kruskemper, H.L. ***Anabolic Steroids***. Academic Press, New York: 1968.

Kinney, J. and Leaton, G. ***Loosening the Grip***. C.V. Mosby Company, St. Lois: 1983.

Mittleman, Roger and Wetli, Charles. *Death Caused by Recreational Cocaine Use.* **Journal of American Medical Association**, October 12, 1984, Volume 252, No. 14.

Morrissey, Elizabeth. *Alcohol-Related Problems in Adolescents and Women.* **Postgraduate Medicine**, December 1978, Volume 64, No. 6.

Mothner, Ira and Weitz, Alan. ***How To Get Off Of Drugs***. Rolling Stone Press. Simon and Schuster. New York: 1984.

Neuman, Patricia and Halvorson, Patricia. ***Anorexia Nervosa and Bulimia, A Handbook for Counselors and Therapists***. Reinhold Company, New York: 1983.

Novak, Allen. *The Deliberate Inhalation of Volitile Substances.* **Journal of Psychedelic Drugs**, April-June 1980, Volume 12(2).

Oster, Gerald and Caro, Janice. ***Understanding and Treating Depressed Adolescents and Their Families***. John Wiley and Sons, New York: 1990.

Siegel, Michele and Brisman, Judith and Weinshel, Margot. ***Surviving An Eating Disorder***. Harper and Row, 1988.

Thomas, John. ***Drugs, Athletes, and Physical Performance***. Plenum Medical Book Company, New York: 1988.

Wells, Brian. ***Psychedelic Drugs***. Jason Aronson, New York: 1974.

Yamaguchi, Kazuo and Kandel, Denise. *Patterns of Drug Use from Adolescence to Young Adulthood: II. Sequences of Progression.* **American Journal of Public Health**, July 1984, Volume 74. No. 7.

Notes

Notes

Notes

Notes

Notes

Notes